Elements of Film Editing

Kuldeep Sinha

DEDICATED
To

All those who incognito

toil in the dark to realize the dreams

Contents

Acknowledgement

The book 'Elements of Film Editing' is the culmination of many years of experience I gained in my association with the marvels in various disciplines of film making those included film directors, editors, writers, sound Designers and many more. It has given me an opportunity to delve upon the intricacies of each department during the production of fiction and non -fiction films. It was my privilege to be associated with them as Producer, Director, Writer and Editor myself for more than three decades.

I will be failing in my duty if I don't mention my alma mater the Film and Television Institute of India which taught me the basics of film making in general and Film Editing in particular.

Shri Hrishikesh Mukherjee, the veteran Film Editor and director in Indian Cinema was always my Inspiration who prompted me to be an Editor first and then be a director. I owe my success and achievements as a film maker to this great film maker of his time.

A book on such a complex subject like film Editing cannot be completed without illustrations and references of outstanding film scenes shot and edited by pioneer directors and editors since cinema came in to existence. I bow my head to all those who not only evolved the principles of film editing but gave a direction to the generations of film makers in the world.

Kuldeep Sinha

Elements of Film Editing

About The Author

Kuldeep Sinha is a national award winning Author and film Writer, Editor and Director who has won considerable renowned for his thought provoking films and writings. He has three short story anthologies to his credit: Kashish, Siskiyaan and Dastak. His books on Film making 'Patkatha Lekhan Ke Tatva' (Elements of screen play writing) and Film Nirdeshan (Direction) are equally popular with students of cinema He was conferred the Rajbhasha Shree and the Saraswat Samman at the Ashirwad awards , Hindi Sahitya Samman By the Ministry of Information and broadcasting, Government of India and few others.

He has written, edited, produced and directed more than two hundred short films on a wide variety of subjects from Agriculture to Arts, from Music to Science and from News and current affairs to Educational films. His films have begged several National and International Honors. He was honored with 'Scroll of Honor' for outstanding services towards the welfare and growth of Hindi Talkie Cinema by Indian Organization of Mass Communication and School of Broadcasting & Communication, Mumbai , and the 'Life Time Achievement Award' for contribution in the growth and promotion of Documentary Films by International Centre for Cultural Relations, Mumbai and many more.

Kuldeep Sinha

An Honors graduate from the University of Pune, He also graduated in cinema from the Film and Television Institute of India with a rare flair in Hindi and English equally .He later studied Journalism, Press relations and Management.

His English novels, **'Neither: The Birth of Transgender,'** analyzes the evolution, the turbulences, social, economic and legal discriminations in the lives of transgender people and **'Behind the moving Images'** *attempts to take a realistic yet measured peep in to the lives of stars and their makers and tell us vividly, how darkness overpowers them once the arcs are faded away, albeit unknown to the outside world most of the times, His other book* **'Mohammad Rafi: The Melody Man'** *is a tribute to one of the greatest Playback singer of Indian cinema.* **'Elements of Film Editing'** *is a complement to his earlier books on Cinema –Screen play writing and Direction.*

From the heart

It was my destiny that took me to film institute in Pune, It was only film institute that could open the doors for my entry in to Films. Hailing from Jhansi, a small town of a large state of Uttar Pradesh in India, I always dreamt to be a film writer and director however I was the lone bird chirping this tune in my family amidst descending voices from my siblings and parents as well. The film profession was never considered to be worthy of any social respect in those days when every parent desired their children to be a doctor, engineer or a teacher or get into a government job even if it was to be a clerical one. A secured job was always considered to be the best one and film industry never fitted in this criteria. I was also forced to prepare for pre- medical tests. I felt like running away from home to peruse my interests when I came across an admission Notice for various film courses in film institute. It was a blessing in disguise for me and I applied for admission with the lone support of my elder brother who was convinced about my passion for cinema. It was a rigorous national selection process from a written test to an Interview. It was always some divine power that helped me to clear all the phases for admission and finally I got admission in Film Editing as I had no other choice but it was an irony that I and no one in my family knew what 'film editing' was about, at the most they could relate the role of an Editor with a pen in his hand and a paper on his table like in Print media.

I was groping in the dark with absolutely no idea about the way I was to proceed with the course. I thought, I must be learning the basic elements of film editing in theory and most of the practical session would be 'automatic' or 'mechanical' but I was wrong. Film Editing unlike today was completely manual whether to roll or unroll a film, winding and spooling of celluloid film reels, cutting and joining the film frames with the help of scissor and film cement, a chemical solution to firm up the film joints, running and stopping the running film roll on the Moviola, a machine to view the film and stop on a frame for marking. The Moviola was also used to Lip-synchronize the separate picture and sound tracks and for preparation of number of other sound tracks like sound effects, Music, dubbed dialogues etc. for final recording. The process was not only time consuming and tiring but also damaging the hands which used to get cut by sharp edges of the film strips and burnt with the chemical reactions while it was applied for joints. No hand gloves were allowed for any editing process except at the time of negative cutting to avoid scratches on the film negatives. I was completely dismayed and disappointed with the process. The physical editing process looked more like a labors' job which was done by an editor. The editing job never fitted into my scheme of things which I nurtured for long time. With each passing day I developed dislikes for the work. I never knew if what I was doing was really editing? I was not the only one to have such a feeling about film editing but there were few others too. Incidentally few of them had left the course mid way and returned home after their disillusionment but I was not that lucky to return back as it was me who staked everything including my further studies, relationship with my family members who opposed my film dreams tooth and nails,, my reputation with my peers who were proud of me when I was selected for admission in a prestigious film school of the country, a privilege very few could have therefore I had no alternative than to pursue my stint in the film institute however the days were not sunny for me. I continued as a reluctant student of cinema till one day there was a surprise visit of Shri Hrishikesh Mukherjee, the ace director and a renowned editor in films who was fondly called 'Hrishi da'. I had grown up appreciating his films since my childhood and heard a lot of his editing skills. I decided to meet him but it was not only me, almost everyone wanted to meet him, some wanted to develop their relation for an opening to associate with him once their course was completed, some actors wanted to break the ice for a lead role in his films while few others wanted to begin their career in cinema as his assistants so everybody had a different motive to meet him. I wanted to meet him to ensure if I had taken up the right course. Incidentally I happened to meet him when he was chatting with students after a film show and discussing the film with the students under the wisdom tree, I arrowed my question to him after telling him briefly about my dreams to be a writer and director in cinema.

'If you want to become a good director, be a good editor first,' was his cryptic reply. After this I had no more query to be answered. His short reply was very well edited and was précised. He continued with other students. His one liner was enough for me to inspire and get engaged diligently in my learning editing. I was spared of many unpleasant and unfortunate situations which would have followed his negative answer that it was. My dreams to become a director were not shattered but crippled however I saw a ray of hope to make it big in Bollywood. The veracity of Hrishi Da's words was realized by me only when I landed in Bombay after completing my film schooling. I put my first step forward in direction and later on specialized in shorts and documentary films. While writing scripts for film and short stories I realized how editing helped me in formulating my story line. In fact mental editing started immediately with the concept and spread over to my subject research and subsequently creating visuals on paper. The editing was a tool to firm up the relevant ideas chronologically which was difficult to change later due to the logical positioning of scenes. The structure thus created was as solid as that of bricks and mortar one. 'Editing' imbibed well subconsciously in my mind, in my thought process, in my creativity, in my imagination and ultimately it reflected in my presentations. Without my knowledge, Editing became an automatic creative force of my day to day working. I am now of the firm opinion that Editing is not important only for a theater or a film director but is important for any creative presentation systematically. Editing is not just a mechanical procedure but also an organizer of our thinking process. To organize our thoughts which often go haywire, knowledge of editing is very important, it is more important for a writer and a director who had to pick up the ideas which appeal. The truth of Hrishi da's words was tumbling out one by one.

When I was in film institute studying cinema, I faced a peculiar problem with the reference books we were recommended. Most of these books had illustrations abstracted from foreign films which were not available to us to corroborate what we studied, it resulted in half knowledge gained and half lost therefore I decided to write books on cinema using the illustrations from the popular films which were easily available in the market, preferably in local language to help those who could not lay their hands to the films which sometimes were not even available in film archives.

The book 'Elements of film Editing' deals with the concepts and principles of film Editing irrespective of the formats (celluloid or digital) being used for making a film however for the reference purpose I preferred celluloid format which has international technical standards in practice unlike its digital counterparts. . I am sure the book serves the purpose for which it is written.

The book 'Elements of film Editing' is the culmination of a series of my books on cinema written earlier titled 'Elements of Screen play writing' and 'Film Direction'. These three books complement each other in the book shelves providing a complete overview on film making to film students and film professionals. The books are not just an academic and technical record of knowledge but also share my personal and professional experiences I gained during my career of more than three decades.

Author.

Kuldeep Sinha

CUT -1

Film Editing: an introduction

'What is film Editing?' no other definition has generated as many interpretations as that of Film Editing. Everyone takes the liberty to interpret it with his narrow understanding, some call it 'Rejecting unwanted shots and put them in order of the story' while some call it 'Acceptability of film shots'. Some people relate it to the more popular concept of Editing of news papers and periodicals which 'compiles the written materials received from different writers and dumps the rest which does not find a place in the news print' however In this case the unused material may not be a waste but it is not used due to its irrelevance to the content, it's topicality and time bound importance. These interpretations reflect general ignorance about the concept and purpose of Editing whether it is for print material or the film material. My purpose here is not to devote more space for discussions on the differences and comparisons in editing procedures for print media or visual media which includes primarily film and television but to guide the students and professionals of cinema who restrict the 'Film Editing' to its mere technical procedures and within the space limits of an Editing room. The editing is beyond the limited scope as perceived by people in general and film professionals in particular.

A film Editor is just not a cutter and joiner but he is the most creative person in the film crew who holds the keys of a 'good film'. A well shot film can be ruined by an unimaginative editor and a 'poorly shot' film can be made interesting by the editor's vision. The job of an editor can best be compared with that of a chef who with the best ingredients at his disposal prepares delicious and lip licking delicacies by utilizing his innovative skills combined with proper quantity of ingredients and timing of heating or cooling the stuff while other may spoil the taste by his lack of knowledge, innovation and dedication.

Editing of a film cannot be confined to the role and responsibilities of an editor but it begins at the moment a writer picks up his pen to scribble his idea of a film and extended to the director, cameramen, sound recordist and sound editor to other technicians in the crew however no serious efforts have been made in the past to define the exact scope of editing for other technicians therefore the entire process of editing has been confined to the editor's table which is aesthetically not correct. Delinking the process of editing from other technicians including the director is not only an injustice to the poor guy called the 'Film Editor' but also wrongly absolves them to share their legitimate responsibility putting an unnecessary burden and onus of making a good film only on the Editor. This is important to know that a poorly shot film by an inefficient technical crew can hardly make a good film on editing table with qualitatively poor ingredients even if an editor splits his hair and breaks his head on the walls therefore it is always not proper to blame an editor for 'bad editing' or a 'bad film' therefore it can be rightly surmised that 'if a film is good, everybody involved is responsible and if a film is bad , it is only the director who is responsible for the fiasco' and he should be ready to share the blame for the reasons that 'A director is considered to be the captain of the ship' and it is his responsibility to sail or sink the ship.

With the above arguments, it will not be appropriate to limit the process of film editing so there cannot be a definite definition. Editing a film is not the beginning of a creative process but its culmination. Broadly film editing can be defined as' An arrangement of shots in the chronological order and timing envisaged in a story or screen play,' but it can be at best be said to be only a physical process that began with the advent of silent cinema when the film editing was limited to physically cutting and joining the shots of various activities and events in chronological order for a continuous projection of the film. In the coming paragraphs, I will concentrate more on the evolution and development of editing process than to talk about machines and tools of Editing which have seen a regular and gradual technical transformation from silent era to the time when sound became an important aspect of film making and the technology will continue to move on.

Editing and silent cinema:

Film editing transforms an illusion in to the creative realism with the help of moving images recorded on the raw stock of picture negative and sound tapes during the shooting of a film. This transformation takes place by the selection of proper images, proper timing and proper placement of shots in

Kuldeep Sinha

chronological order of the script to provide an illusion of a real action in continuity.

The advent of silent cinema in the late nineteenth century was in fact the capturing of real activities or events in a single shot by Lumiere brothers without a preconceived idea or a story line or a rehearsal by the performers. The purpose of these films was to entertain the captive audience by projecting the reality on celluloid film through moving pictures. The movies were a step forward from the earlier still photography. These single shot films by the lumiere brothers included, 'A train leaving the station', 'Baby at the lunch table', ' A boat leaving the harbour' and many more. The entire action was generally covered without a cut. Where there were more than one cuts in the action, each shot was cut and pasted together in such a way that entire action looked like a single continuous action but these multiple cuts were absolutely not planned and preconceived. The purpose of the multiple cuts was to present the movement in the most realistic manners maintaining the continuity of actions.

After experimenting with the 'presentation of reality' the Lumiere brothers moved one more step ahead to 'create an action' and pre plan the shoot in the film 'Watering the garden'. A gardener is shown watering the plants in a garden with a rubber pipe. A cute baby enters and puts his foot on the pipe stopping the flow of water. The gardener is surprised at the sudden stoppage of the water. When gardener looks at him, he leaves the pipe and water wets the gardener. Seeing he wet, the child starts laughing.' This was the first experiment in the history of silent cinema by the Lumiere brothers to make a film with the sole purpose to entertain people with a preconceived story and pre planed action.

Following the footsteps of Lumiere brothers in the film 'Watering the garden', George Melies did another experiment of creating special visual effects or trick photography wherever required in the camera itself while shooting a film, putting a halt in the practice of taking a scene in a single shot. This had enhanced the possibilities of better story telling including special effects to make the film more interesting and entertaining. While the single shot series of films by Lumieres did not exceed the length of more than 50 ft each, the film 'Cinderella' (1899) made by George Melies was much longer to the length of 410ft.. The 'Cinderella' was shot in the series of 20 parts, each part of the film was similar to the one-shot films of Lumieres however every part of Cinderella' was inter connected with other to take the story forward unlike the films of Lumiere brothers which were complete in a single shot. Revolving around a single character of Cinderella, the film had a definite story line with each part having a different title such as, 'Cinderella in her kitchen', 'The ferry, mice and Leaches',' The triumph of Cinderella' etc. 'Cinderella' was the beginning of fiction films based on a preconceived story with characters and preplanned shooting style engaging actors to play the characters in a film. In subsequent years more experimentation was carried out for a better and effective story telling.

In another landmark experiment Melies used his camera as an audience. The way people sitting in front watch an action played on the stage in a theatrical production, Melies fixed his camera among them to cover an action on a fixed background. In 'Cinderella' and other productions of George Melies, though there was a continuity of story content, it was missing in context of the background, actions, continuity from one shot to another, Timing etc. captions were used in between the shots to carry forward the story idea. Influenced by the theatre, these films were close to one 'act' in a stage play therefore it was clear that Melies' style was highly influenced by the theatre.

Edwin S. Porter, the first cameraman of Edison virtually revolutionized the style, presentation and technique of film making in 1902 by his film' The life of an American fireman'. Porter was mesmerized by the actions and dare devilry of 'Fire fighters'. He shot an entire operation of fire fighting undertaken by the fire station. While the coverage was very effective, it lacked elements of interest and entertainment for the audience. He needed a story to make the film entertaining therefore he introduced characters of a mother and a child who was trapped in fire and a rescue operation to save them was shot accordingly. The operation was divided in number of unrelated shots which individually did not convey anything but when joined together chronologically, they produced a different meaning taking forward the story of the mother and her child who were trapped in fire and recued. 'The life of an American fireman' was a remarkable mix of reality coverage and dramatic enactments which kept its audience spellbound till the trapped family were rescued for their utter relief.

'The life of an American fireman'-

Defying his predecessors of shooting an entire scene in a single shot without a cut, Porter conceived a dramatic sequence having multiple shots as under, covering the scene from different perspectives and backgrounds maintaining the continuity of thoughts and action of fire fighting and rescue operation, giving human touch with an emotional appeal by introducing the characters of a mother and a child who were trapped in the fire in a building to make the film more gripping and interesting.

- The crew of fire brigade moves in to the place where fire is broke out.
- A building is in flames.
- In the background, the fire van enters in speed and stops.
- Orders are given to fix the engine. Water pipes are taken out of the van.
- Stairs are fixed on the windows of the building.
- Water is gushed with speed through hose pipes on the fire spots. (Dissolve to)
- In the interior of the building a mother with her baby are entrapped in the fire and smoke.
- They run around to save themselves but fail.
- They feel suffocated amidst the fire and smoke.
- The lady shouts from the window to appeal the surging crowd to save them.
- She is again entrapped in the smoke and a burning log falls on the bed in the room.
- A fire man (The Hero) breaks open the door with the help of a spade to enter the room.
- He tears the drapers and opens the windows of the room. He orders his other colleagues to put up a stair on the window.
- Immediately a stair comes up to the window.

- The hero lifts the lady on his shoulder like a gunny bag and climbs down with her on the stair. (The scene is dissolved to).
- Exterior of the building is seen burning.
- Lady in her night suit regains her consciousness and requests the hero to save her child.
- Hero calls his men to follow him and returns back with them to bring the child safely.
- He enters into the room through the window. Tension is built up for some time giving a presumption that the hero himself is trapped in the fire and smoke and it was difficult for him to come back alive. After some time he is seen holding the child in his arms.
- He comes down and hands over the child to his mother ending the breathtaking climax to a happy end.

The story is conceived and divided very intelligently in three parts to approach the climax. First part is the establishment of a problem that is the eruption of fire in a residential building. The flames increase with the flow of the wind. Another part consists of a mother and a child who is entrapped in the fire and smoke and is fighting to save themselves. The third part is the entry of the Hero who risks his own life and daringly gets in to the fire scene and rescues the lady and her child bringing relief to them and the onlookers. The continuity in the action has been maintained by joining shots in chronological order to give a feeling of a continuous fire fighting and rescue operation. The film ends with the resolution of the problem when a lady and her child are saved.

If we take a close look at the difference in the style of film making of both these pioneer film makers, George Melies and Edwin S. porter, we can easily point out that if George Melies would have made the film 'The life of an American Fireman', he would have separated these parts with a Title caption in between to proceed with the story but Porter has treated every shot as a 'unit' of a continuous action and joined them to carry forward the story without a jerk or a visual distraction. He had reversed the concept of telling one point at a time in a single shot. This has given greater advantage of creative freedom to a director. The continuity of the events or action in the scene presented an illusion of reality to the audience for a better emotional connect and grasp. In 'The life of an American fireman' Porter had beautifully combined the reality and theatrical enactments without disrupting the continuity of a story line and action. This was the beginning of 'Fiction film' making of today. It is another point that modern film makers concoct the reality the way they want to see it and want their audience to see it the same way.

Another advantage of assembling number of shots to a definite story line is that director can establish the event by squeezing the duration of the whole action which is also accepted by the viewers. 'In the life of an American fireman' the entire action of fire fighting and rescue operations was contracted to less than 10 minutes of the real time of many hours however the audience was given the psychological feeling of the event in real time. In this film Porter has proved the following points very effectively-

1. No single shot can be complete in action.
2. A shot is only a small 'unit' of the entire scene. The

way bricks are properly fixed   together one by one with another to erect a wall or a building, proper placement of shots when joined together create a scene or a film. This is the first principle of editing.

This basic principle of editing was followed more precisely and systematically by Porter in his next film,' The Great train robbery' in the year 1903. Known for innovative approach, the 'one shot transition' was another innovation carried out by Porter in the film. In 'one shot transition' technique an action was divided into many shots and in editing the action was completed by joining shots in the chronological order in the similar manner as we climb up the ladder step by step. This is called single shot transition which was never used earlier by anybody.

The Great train robbery-

Scene 9- Panoramic view of the valley. A group of robbers is running on the horses.

Scene 10- In the telegraph room, the operator with his hands and legs tied by ropes tries hard to reach to his telegraph table but falls down unconscious. His little daughter brings food for him. She cuts his ropes and throws water on his face to bring him to consciousness. He becomes conscious. Fresh with the memories of the robbery he comes out of the room to give alarm.

Scene 11- People are dancing in a hall. The door opens and the telegraph operator enters in semi conscious state. The dance stops and few people come out with their rifle.

'The great train robbery' was technically one step ahead of

'The life of an American fireman' due to 'different actions' occurring at the same time in two different locations showed simultaneously. This is called **'Parallel action'.** 'The great train robbery' was a very simplistic narration with effective use of continuity of action' 'and 'parallel action' to convey a story effectively however his presentation had its own inherent limitations as his events were never preplanned, picked up haphazardly and were shot in theatre style keeping the camera at a fixed distance. This restricted the observation and control by the director over the events and actions. It was on the actors to convey the meaning to the audience through their actions, mannerism and expressions. This technique had direct influence of the theatre in its execution.

Almost after twelve years D.W.Griffith had liberally used this technique of parallel actions in his films. He not only accepted and executed the techniques developed by Porter but also improved them. His creative experiments became mile stones in the history of cinema. To understand Griffith, let's have a look on the scenes and shot composition from the reel no.6 of his film, 'The Birth of a Nation'-

Film-The Birth of a Nation: Assassination of Lincoln.

Benjamin Cameron comes out of 'stoneman House' with his friend Essle stoneman. They move to a theatre to see a special performance which was also to be attended by President Lincoln. The performance in the theatre has started.

Title: Arrival of the President

Location: Auditorium

1.F.S. Full Shot. Interior, staircase,

The security guards of President Lincoln climb the stairs of the auditorium one after another to take their positions at the **president's enclosure. After some time president arrives.**

2.Interior, President's box.

President's box is seen from inside. His security men guard the box.

3.Full Shot, President's box, Exterior,

President removes his hat and gives to his assistant.

4.Interior, President's box as in shot 2.

Lincoln enters in to his box.

5.Mid shot, Interior, Theatre,

Essley and Ben are sitting in the theatre. They turn to see the president and get up to clap for him.

6.F.S.stage in the long shot. President's box is on the right.

The audience stand up and turn to clap and welcome the president.

7.Interior, President's box as in shot 2.

Lincoln and his wife bow to thank people.

8.Long shot of the stage as in shot 6.

9.President's box. As in shot 7.

Mr. and Mrs, Lincoln take their seats after thanking the audience.

10.Full shot. Exterior, President's box,

President's security guards come out of the box and take their place. One of them scratches his knee.

11.Full shot. View of the stage from rear.

The performance on stage continues.

12.President's box, as in shot 9.

Lincoln holds the hands of his wife while seeing the performance.

13.F.S. View from the rear. As in shot 11.

Audience stop clapping.

14.Close shot of the stage.

Actors are performing.

15.F.S.Security guards as in shot 10.

A guard feels uncomfortable.

16.C.S.of the stageas in shot 14.

Performance is continued on the stage.

17.F.S.guards as in shot 15.

The guard in shot 15 shifts his chair behind the door.

18.interior President's box as in shot 6.

Camera is near the box. The guard returns to his place.

19.Close shot of the box nearer than shot 18.

The guard sits in his place.

Scene 2 ,Act-3. Assassination. Time -10.30. p.m.,

20. F.S of the hall, Stage view from the rear.

Lincons box is seen through a mask.

21.M.S. Essley and Ben in the hall.

Essley shows something to Ben towards Lincoln's box.

22. Face of John Booth through the mask.

23.M.S Essley and Ben as in shot 21.

Essley enjoys the performance.

24.M.S. Booth in mask as in shot 22,

Face of John Booth in Mask.

25.C.S. Lincoln'sBox.

Lincoln watches the program.

26.M.S. Booth in mask as in shot 22.

Face of john Booth.

27. C.S. Stage,

Actors are performing.

28. C.S. Lincoln's box as in shot 25.

Lincoln smiles while watching the act. feeling chilled he pulls up his coatand wears it.

29. M.S. Booth as in shot 22.

Booth looks up to get up.

30.C.S. Lincoln's box. Interior,

Lincoln watches the program.

31.F.S. Rear view of the stage as in shot 20.

Full shot. Mask is removed to show full view of the hall.

32.C.S Security guards behind the circular mask as in shot 19.

33.F.S.Booth

Booth exits from the door to come near to Lincoln. He peeps through the hole., takes out his pistol and prepares for the next action.

34.C.S. of the pistol.

35. Shot 33 continues.

Booth comes near the door and opens it with some difficulty and enters in to Lincoln's box.

36.C.S. Lincoln's box as in shot 25.

Booth stands behind Lincoln.

37.Stage as in shot 14.

Actors perform.

38. Lincoln's Box as in shot 36.

Booth fires at Lincoln from the back. Lincoln falls down unconscious. Booth escapes from the side and jumps out.

39.L.S. Booth reaches to the stage.

Booth screams on the stage.

The story of 'The Birth of a nation' revolves around President Lincoln, carelessness of his Guards and his assassin John Booth. This simple story has been dramatized and presented effectively which not only entertains people but keeps them on their toes waiting for the next course of the action. Porter might have finished this film in few shots but Griffith has very intelligently divided the entire story into four parts for which appropriate characters were conceived, prominent of them were the President Lincoln and His wife, President's Guards, assassin John Booth, Essley stoneman and Ben Cameron. The group of performers are created for ambience and some dramatic effect in the auditorium although it seems that the group of performers is distracting the attention from the main event but in reality it is not so as the performance on the stage extends the excitement and built up tension that keeps audience glued to their seats so the performance too become a part of the dramatization. This makes the presentation more interesting and entertaining. While doing this Griffith has taken due care of principles of continuity which he has never broken.. He has also used parallel actions to show simultaneous happenings in different locations but at the same time, Parallel actions are imbibed with the main story so well that they assimilate with the theme very effectively without diluting the flow of the main story. Griffith has also experimented with the technique of intercutting which means dividing a shot many pieces and using them at different places.

The difference in the working style of both Porter and Griffith is that Porter has divided his action into many shots because it was not possible for him to cover the entire action or incident in one single shot due to its duration and magnanimity but Griffith has deliberately conceived a story and characters in many parts to build up the excitement and dramatized the presentation in which ambience played an important role. The ambience helped the audience to be an integral witness of the story and happenings around. This is a great accomplishment of Griffith which separates him and Porter. However Porter's contribution and innovation to deal with a situation that forced him to divide his action in to many shots cannot be undermined. Porter's technique was adopted and improved upon by Griffith that took him one more step to advance cinematic creativity. With number of shots at his disposal for Editing, Griffith acquired extra liberty to be more innovative and experimental. While accepting Porter's traditions Griffith has added new ones in his urge for extraordinary experimentation in cinematic productions.

In the film 'The Birth of a Nation' the director has worked successfully on many deferent aspects to obtain a cumulative effect. Griffith has divided the whole action into many components to recreate a scene. With this he has been able to touch the depth in the story telling or the narration which had long lasting emotional effect on audience's mind. The detailed description and interpretation of the scene enhances the realism and brings the audience close to their personal experiences which is difficult to achieve in one single shot. Another advantage of having multiple shots in a scene is that the Director is able to conveniently manipulate audience's reaction to the ongoing events by associating characters' actions and reactions by linking them with the main events of the story. The viewer thus starts associating himself with the characters on the screen and becomes himself a character in the situation. Lets analyze 'The birth of a Nation' to understand this factor appropriately.

'The Birth of a Nation' – an analysis:

Scene: The assassination of Lincoln.

- First fourteen shots in the film show the President arriving to the theatre and his welcome by the people present there. A caption inserted here is an indication of some forthcoming danger.

- Next five shots are similar to Porter's single shot action that show various actions of the guard, Like scratching his knee, feeling of boredom etc. in the shot no 15 the Guard is feeling uncomfortable, instead of 'what will he do or not do' scene shifts to the performance on the stage which the Guard wants to watch but cannot due to his posting that's why he moves to the door of the theatre in shot no17, 18, 19 but returns back to his place. This does not in any way distracts the mood and attention from the main event and continuity is maintained properly. In shot 17 and 18 the guards goes up to the door to see the action on the stage but fails to see it and returns back in shot 18 and 19 to create drama. Another caption in this place reflects ignorance of the audience about impending danger.

- In shot nos.20-30 the Director heightens the suspense by showing mysterious activities of John Booth. An attempt has been made to prolong the suspense by interrupting Booth's mysterious activities with other happenings in the auditorium. Thereafter Booth is projected like an ordinary man so that there is no doubt about him. After some time Booth takes advantage of the Guard who once again left his place and Booth plans his further action as shown in shot no.33-36.

- Once again action in shot 36 is interrupted to show actors' performance in shot no.37 thereafter continuation of shot no 36 is shown in shot no 38. Shot no 37 does not show anything new but enhances the dramatic effect of the scene. Suspense and horrification has been prolonged artificially leaving the President unaware of the impending danger therefore in Griffith's editing Drama is created in very extended and simplistic form to avoid uneasiness and artificiality for the viewers.

- In shot no.21 Essley pointing out at the Lincoln that hints for something coming up as if Essley has seen the assassin and presumes a mishap. The audiences thus look at Essley with some hopes that he would take some action to prevent the mishap. In reality this shot of Essley has no meaning in the scene but it helps in increasing the suspense and drama. Before the assassin fires at the Lincoln, though the President is unaware of the future events, it seems that he inadvertently could do something to avoid the unforeseen occurrence but it does not happen. His actions are considered to be his normal activities before he is murdered.

Griffith had realized that Porter's single shot taking technique in which camera was placed at a fixed distance to shoot like a stage performance, had its own limitations. In this style the viewers could only see the events from the perspective of a fixed distance. Actions performed from other variable distances may not be visible so the actions and reactions of other performers at varied distances were not possible to register in Porter's technique. To solve this issue Griffith had divided the entire scene into many fragments (shots) and while shooting each fragment he decided the actions and reactions of the performers to be covered by placing the camera at variable distances as per the dramatic and horripilate requirements of the scene. He placed the camera close to actors to cover their minute reactions. Like wise to establish a location and the ambience, he placed the camera at long distance for a wider view. Thus 'Long shots' (L.S.) and 'Close shots' (C.S.) were discovered during the shooting. In this technique the freedom and convenience to place the camera anywhere in between was also acquired. The use of Long shots, even the unrelated to the plot, by Griffith helped creating better dramatics   improving the technical quality of the scene. Another important innovation by Griffith was the use of **'Flash back'** which became an important vehicle to convey actors' emotional state, memories of the past and events, his ideas and thoughts to the audience. Griffith experimented with this technique freely in his next film **'Intolerance'**. He mixed 'flash back' shots with the present one very simply to relate the present with the past. In such combinations narrative continuity of the story is more important than the physical continuity.

The greatest advantage of fragmenting a scene into many shots was that the director is not dependent on shooting the entire scene in a single shot nor he has to wait for the entire performance to take place at a time as the actions could be decided as per the requirement of the scene irrespective of the magnanimity and the duration of the scenes like war scene or a gathering or a celebrations or a protest and procession etc. Everything could be shot in fragments with short enactments/actions as required in the shot however it made a bit difficult for performers to act in close shots; they were so far used to act for an audience sitting at a distance where they could hardly see their minute facial expressions. While Close shots were difficult for the actors, their effect on the audience was immense. In Porter's single shot technique actors had to indulge in overacting or loud acting to make an impact on viewers sitting at a distance. With the innovation of Griffith's techniques while the job of actors became more difficult, the responsibility to create dramatic effects had fallen on the shoulders of the directors. In 'The Birth of a Nation' the suspense regarding Lincon's assassination became more effective with the repeated use of shot no.37 than with the performance of actors. Therefore it is the Director who has to decide how and where a shot has to be used to make the scene more effective and thrilling. The impact of a shot is not as dependent on the actors' performance as it is on the talent, merit and creative acumen of the director how he uses it. Similarly how and where the camera is to be placed, at what angle and composition shot has to be taken and   how actors move in their actions are better predefined by the director.

The pertinent question that arises with the use of multiple shots is that how long a shot should remain on the screen and who decides it? Normally it is a joint decision of the Director and the Editor. In this context I would like to add a thumb rule that if the scene has to be fast paced, the length of the shots will be shorter and opposite to this if it is a slow moving scene then the shots will be lengthy. The duration of a visual on the screen is directly proportionate to the length of the shot as the universal speed with which a film strip runs on the projector is 24 frames/sec. Generally action oriented scenes have faster rate of editing /cutting of the shots (shorter shots /less duration) than the dialogue scenes (lengthy shots/longer duration). The rhythm (speed) of the entire film is determined by the Director based on the content and requirements of the scenes as there s no formula for determining the speed of the film.

Griffith very successfully adopted the style of a story teller while narrating his films. The way a story teller engages dramatic elements to sustain the interest of the audience from beginning to end including mannerism of actors, their actions and reactions, ambience etc. and approach to the climax, Griffith too employed the use of Long shots, Mid shots and close shots to provide variety of visual actions and emotions to the viewers to engage them till the end. That's where Griffith has surpassed Porter and he is called 'The father of Editing'.

It was not that in other parts of the world there was no experimentation in film production. Russian film maker Sergei Eisenstein had quoted about Griffith in his article 'Dicans, Griffith and the film today', 'Griffith has used literary style in his editing technique and translated the conventions of storytelling of a novelist in his films. Cross cuttings, close shots, flash backs and dissolves too have parallels in the literature which were discovered by Griffith'.

Griffith had impressed many Russian film makers of the time but they also pointed out certain flaws in his technique such as his use of Close shots only for 'Parallel actions' while Russians have used various shots to make a **'Montage'** which had a different meaning and effect than the meaning and effect of individual shots. According to this experiment 'when more than one shots are joined together they have different meaning and effect than that of the original shots.' Its parallel can be found in 'Figure of speech' in the literature where every word or Phrase when combined with others gives a different meaning. A figure of speech is a word or phrase that has a meaning something different than its literal meaning. It can be a metaphor or simile that is designed to further explain a concept. Or, it can be a different way of pronouncing a word or phrase such as with alliteration to give further meaning or a different sound. This similarity is evident in the 'Montage' where unrelated shots mean differently when joined together.

There were no 'Montages' in Griffith's technique. His close shots, ambience, traits of actors/characters etc were used as an alternative to the dialogues of the main actors. In chase sequences close shots of chaser and chased were alternately used to speed up the pace of the scene and increase the thrill and not for increasing the importance or visual effects of the scene by 'Juxtapositions' of the shots differently. Since the films made by Griffith were in incessant years of their development, his limited use of the shots should not be underrated but it should be accepted as another step in the growth of cinematic techniques. Subsequent film makers after Griffith not only used shots as a tool for story narration but also experimented for developing new Editing techniques and deriving newer interpretations, intellectual meanings and effects.

According to Eisenstein, the film making in Russia was limited to the advertisement films to promote products and political ideology. Film production was not an organized industry at that time which restricted the knowledge, vision and imagination of film makers in Russia. Griffith's techniques and inventions have provided them an opportunity to think and explore the possibilities of development of films in their country. They picked up the basic theory of film editing from Griffith and worked to develop newer techniques and principles. Neo film makers used film as medium to propagate their ideas among them **'Pudovkin'** and **'Kuleshov'** marked their presence in golden letters in the history of cinema.

Pudovkin:

Pudovkin worked to rationalize the basic principles of film making propounded by Griffith. While Griffith believed in resolution of the problems as per his needs, Pudovkin had preempted and assessed the issues to develop a new working systems which are very important to the contemporary film makers even today. Pudovkin had formulated the guiding principles and systems of editing for the generations of film makers.

To understand Pudovkin's principles of Editing, we have to analyze the role of a Director. Apparently a scene shot in fragments (shots) by the director are not more than unorganized and incomplete pieces of celluloid strip which have no meaning as they don't convey anything individually. These shots are taken to cover different actions from different viewpoints and perspectives which are not conveyed. It is like an arrangement of words that makes a sentence which has a meaning than that of the individual words used haphazardly in it without a meaning and communicates nothing. Similar words in different sentences convey different meanings. In the same manners each shot is only a fragment of an action and not a whole action. Therefore the exposed raw material brought by the director in fragmented form does not present a complete action, its timing and locations. These shots have to be organized systematically as per the editorial principles and practices to create a meaningful scene which depends on the imagination, merits and creativity of the Editor or the Director of editing. While giving these shots a 'film form', unwanted actions and reactions, various intervals and gaps are removed. The Editor has a liberty to decide about the timing of a shot to remain on the screen as per the requirements of the scene. This is called 'Constructive Editing' as per Pudovkin's principles of Editing. The creative or constructive editing can be understood by the following example .Many times we are awed to see a character jumping from a height of a tower or so but the Director pictures this action as under…

First of all in shot 1, the actor jumps from the height on a net spread down below. This net is not seen on the screen. In the second shot, the actor jumps from a lesser height to the ground. Both the shots are joined together in such a way that the action from top to the ground is seen continuous one. Therefore it is not a real dangerous action of jumping from a height to the ground as it looks but is an outcome of editorial juxtaposition to create an emotional impact. Special attention is given to maintain the continuity of action by deleting unwanted intervals and gaps, waiting or getting up of the character etc. It is not a photographic trick or special effect but a presentation of an action by using editorial practices. Now a days such actions are created digitally with special effects.

Pudovkin has converted Griffith's Editing practices in to Principles of editing. Griffith's use of Close shots to create a dramatic effect was completely different than Pudovkin's fragmentation of the scene into shots for creating the same, what we call now is a 'pre shooting shot division' which is followed by the Director during the shoots. Thus the editorial process for a director starts with the beginning of screen play writing itself. For example-

Scene -1:

'A horse cart of a farmer is moving slowly on a muddy pathway of a countryside village. The cart is stuck in the mud. The disgusted farmer pushes his tired horse to move ahead. At a distant corner of the cart a human shape emerges out of the dust storm. She wraps her clothes around to protect herself from the wind and dust, the passerby stops near the horse cart and looks at it amazingly.

The farmer turns to asks him, **'Is Nakhabin far away from here?' (caption)**

The man guides him pointing to the direction. The cart starts moving again. The man looks at the cart for some time and moves on to his route.'

The screen play is generally written in the above format. Since there were no dialogues in cinema in those days, scenes were separated by inserting captions in between the scenes. Director's comments or views about the scene/theme were also captioned in proper places. In the above example it is observed that actions and reactions are minutely detailed like cart's trap in the mud, disgusted farmer, tired horse, emergence of a human shape at a distant corner, wrapping of her clothes around to protect her from dust and gusty wind, surprise of the passerby etc. These details are similar to that of a literary writer creating a visual presentation in his story or a novel with the sole objective of taking his readers to the illusion of actuality from where he could feel the impact of the scene. The writer and the director of a film too have the same objective when they write a screen play. This is the time when the editing pattern of the film is also outlined. The shot division of the above scene would be somewhat like this-

1. Long shot- A farmer on his sores cart going on a muddy path.
2. Close shot- The cart wheel sticks in the mud.
3. Mid shot- The cart moves slowly.
4. Close shot- Farmer is disgusted.

5.   Mid shot- The farmer pushes his tired horse to move faster.

6.   Long shot- The cart in the foreground. A human figure emerges at a distance.

7.   Mid shot- she wraps her clothes around to protect from the gusty winds.

8.   Long shot- A passer by stops near the cart.

9.   Close shot- He looks at the cart with surprise.

10.   Close shot- The farmer turns to him and asks:

11.   Caption- 'Is Nakhabin far away from here?'

12.   Mid shot- The man guides him to a direction.

13.   Long shot- The cart starts moving again.

14.   Close shot- The man looks at the cart moving away for a while.

15.   Long shot- He moves forward on his way.

It is amply clear from the above shot division of the scene that minute details and facial expressions must be shown in C.S. or M.S.so that the viewers can experience the same feelings which would not be possible if the entire scene is shot in Long shots. Though viewers will be able to see the event in Long shot but the appropriate expressions and their effect on them will be missed out. According to Pudovkin every shot in a scene should have different effect and meaning unlike in a monotonous Long shot which is occasionally punctuated with close shots or mid shots to show the details. Such shots neither serve any creative or dramatic purpose or reason nor contribute in creative editing therefore they should be removed. These inferences of Pudovkin were based on some of his own experiences and some on the experiments of Kuleshov in the process of editing which he considered was more important in story telling than the visuals.

Kuleshov:

According to Kuleshov's theory, 'By proper juxtaposition a new meaning or interpretation of shots can be derived which is not conveyed by original shots". This can be easily understood by the following example-

Shot No. 1.   Smiling face of the Hero.

Shot No.2.   A revolver.

Shot No. 3.   Frightened face of the Hero.

When we look at the above shots in the same order, we see that the Hero is frightened when he sees the revolver. This explains that the Hero is a weak hearted person and his frightened face reflects his cowardice.

Shot No. 1.   Frightened face of the Hero.

Shot No.2.   A revolver.

Shot No. 3.   Smiling face of the Hero.

In the reverse order when we see his frightened face first and subsequently the revolver and his smiling face in the above order, A frightened Hero looks at the Revolver and smiles giving impression of his daring nature who feels happy with a revolver. Just by reversing the order of the shot we have been able to change the character and his behavior completely. It gives another meaning and effect of the scene to the viewers. Otherwise all these three shots individually have no meaning but when they are juxtaposed differently they convey differently. Thus the director can create the required meaning and effect just by deferring the order of the shots. This is called 'Creative Editing.'

In another experiment Pudovkin and Kuleshov juxtaposed three different close shots with a neutral shot of the Hero intercut in between.

First shot-   C.S.   A Bowl of soup is kept on a table.

Second shot-   C.S.   A lady lay wrapped in a funeral cloth.

Third shot-   C.S.   A baby is playing with her toys.

When the audience was shown these three shots in combination with the Hero's neutral shots, their reaction was astounding.

First shot-   Close shot of Hero

Second shot-   A lady laid wrapped in a funeral cloth.

Third shot-   Close shot of Hero

Fourth shot-   A Bowl of soup is kept on a table.

Fifth shot-   Close shot of Hero

Sixth shot-   A baby is playing with her toys.

Seventh shot-   Close shot of Hero

When the Hero looks at the lady in funeral cloth, the pathetic reaction of the hero was heart touching. Seeing the lady dead, hero forgot to have the soup kept for him on the table. When he saw the baby playing with her toys, he felt happy. The viewers appreciated Hero's versatile performance in these combinations without realizing that all these shots of the Hero were neutral and devoid of any expressions but part of the same shot (used four times). An intelligent juxtaposition and intercutting gave different interpretation and emotional context to the shots.

There has to be basic material for any creative work which is arranged systematically, according to Kuleshov,' for a Musician or composure 'sound' is the base material which is composed in particular rhythm and pace. For a Painter' his 'colors' are the basic material which he arranges on a canvas. Similarly for a film maker the shots of the exposed film are the basic material which are joined creatively to produce an effective and interesting scene.' Kuleshov opined that 'Film art does not begin with the performance of an actor or with the completion of shooting as this is only a basic procedure to prepare the basic material. The film art begins when a Director starts joining the shots and achieves the desired effect after many permutations and combination of shots.'

Griffith and Pudovkin - a comparison:

The difference between the Editing techniques of Pudovkin and Griffith was in the level of emotional impact of the scene. Griffith used to concentrate more on the behavior, movements and mannerism of actors while Pudovkin worked on the details in the shots to incorporate more variety and dramatic effect. It was predominantly achieved through creative juxtaposition of shots. His technique is still followed by many film makers today. Griffith played more on human conflicts and Pudovkin emphasized more on ambience of the story and the surrounding events. Pudovkin worked on simple plots based on common events where he devoted more screen time to explain the pros and cons and justify their importance.

Film- Mother   Director: Pudovkin

'Mother' is another example of a good '**continuity**' of scenes and experiment in juxtaposition of unrelated shots to establish the pleasure of a man who is about to be released from the prison. Pudovkin has presented the scene very effectively. According to his own statement, 'In **Mother** I have tried to impress my audience with the psychological state of my characters along with some experiments in editing. The son is sitting in jail when he is handed over a piece of paper in which it is written that he will be released from the custody next day. I had a problem to show his facial expressions of happiness when he gets this information. Normally, to show him smiling would have not been effective. Therefore First I had shown his trembling hands followed by a big close up of his lower half of the face to include a corner of his lips with a short smile. I had juxtaposed these shots with few unrelated shots of different ambience like shots of brooks, spring flowers, sunrays falling on water, birds playing in a village pond and a laughing child. In this way by juxtaposing few different shots, I could establish the pleasure on the face of the prisoner'.

When the scene is analyzed, it does not seen to be effective apparently but the director wanted it this way. Showing just a smiling face of the actor would not have the desired impact director wanted to create. He took the help of those elements of nature which expressed happiness therefore the Director juxtaposed those pleasure symbols from the nature to create a 'Montage' where physically every shot seemed directly disconnected but each of them had indirect ideological link which expressed a definite emotion.

According to Pudovkin,' if the details of an event in the scene are fragmented and joined creatively, they produce tremendous effect on the audience.' But Sergei Eisenstein had a different view. He believed that,' linking of various shots depicting details of a scene is very normal. To achieve continuous interest and regular flow in the film, it is necessary to incorporate elements of shocks and surprises at regular intervals. With every cut audience must be provided an opportunity to experience 'conflict' and anticipate further possibilities of 'what next'.

Every shot of a 'Montage' should indicate forthcoming shocks and surprises. Such juxtapositions in editing help achieve the thrill. Eisenstein imagines 'Intellectual Montage' when he compares cinema with other art forms. The intellectual Montage can be understood like this:

Shot of Dripping water + eyes	=	Sense of crying.
Shot of an ear + close to door	=	Sense of Hearing.
A Dog + face	=	Sense of Barking.
A face + Child	=	Sense of shrieking.
A face + a Bird	=	Sense of singing.
A knife + a Heart	=	Sense of sorrow.

For Eisenstein such '**Intellectual Montage**' is cinema in which each shot has a different meaning and emotion but their content is always 'Neutral'. When these shots are juxtaposed together in an intellectual context a series intellectual interpretations is formed. Director should choose his shots conflicting with each other and proceed further incorporating inherent meanings and emotions of the shots in the content to provide his audience an opportunity to feel shocked and surprised. These shocks and surprises can be created by the variety and contrast in the composition of shots, Distance from the camera, Back ground, Depth of field, cinematographic technology and gimmicks, special lighting arrangements etc. This can also be created by connecting some disconnected shots .The duration of the shock is not so important which can be short or longer as decided by the director.

In the 'Intellectual Montage' of Eisenstein the problem is not that of the juxtaposition of shots but of how easily the viewers will be able to understand its inherent meaning and emotions. It is possible that they may not understand it when they watch it first time or they may have to tax their mind to understand it in many times for which they may not have the time and patience. In such a situation Director may not be able to convey properly what he wants to say. But whatever it may be, by his concept of 'Intellectual Montage' Eisenstein had definitely created a new 'Genre' of film making which can be called' Intellectual or Experimental Cinema'.

*****

Cut - 2

The Development of Editing

The Development of editing could be attributed to the development of Cinema in the world. Porter, Griffith, Pudovkin, Kuleshov, Eisenstein and many more in other countries have contributed with their new concepts, process and technology as per the needs in such a way that cinematography should not merely become coverage of the events. Actions were fragmented into many incomplete shots to enhance director's imagination and creativity to make the scene utmost dramatic and entertaining. Every shot was important and had different meaning when juxtaposed with another. The unique composition of shots had also developed the techniques of cinematography. The history of cinema has been a struggle to work towards effective and dramatic presentation of cinematic scenes. Directors were inspired to think newer ideas and methods to present complicated and emotional plots in exciting manners. With these efforts the development of visual continuity came into practice.

Film editing was not a compulsion for the directors but was an effort to arrange disconnected shots of a scene in a single unified visual action and emotional thought effectively and dramatically. This had resulted in the development of new processes, principles and techniques of editing. Lumiere Brothers did not need editing for their single shot films but when Porter started to film a series of fragmented actions, he needed to link them together. Subsequently Pudovkin had to juxtapose incomplete shots of a scene in different methods for proper continuity and dramatic impact of a scene. Taking forward this tradition Griffith and Eisenstein redefined the whole cinematic concept to intellectual and experimental presentation giving editing a complete new dimension. So we can say that 'Editing is not a technique but a procedure to present a scene effectively which is decided by a director's individual imagination and creativity' therefore there cannot be strict parameters and standards but they can only be the guiding principles for editing. It is said that 'to break a rule one should know the rules', similarly to edit a film an Editor should have the knowledge of these guiding factors.

With the advent of 'sound' in cinema after a long stint of silent movie making, many believed that sounds deteriorated the visual impact while many others were of the view that 'sounds should be used for a limited purpose only to enhance the dramatic effect of a scene.' When films became popular as a medium of entertainment, few producers jumped in to the bandwagon of commercialism and started making entire film with the extensive use of sounds predominately in dialogue sequences. This helped them to narrate a story with more clarity without resorting to the use of captions, a practice which was not avoidable in silent cinema. It has always been difficult for people to accept a big change, similarly many film makers of silent era did not relish ii however many of them were accused of misusing the newly acquired technology to use the sound extensively. It was an irony that if the sounds in cinema would have arrived earlier, film makers would have been deprived of the discoveries, the experiments, the innovations and formulations of the principles of editing propounded by Pudovkin, Griffith and Eisenstein and others. In such a situation it would have been difficult to conceive the form of a film without having benefitted by the principles of editing. In this film form, scenes could be like trees of different shapes and sizes, flowers, leaves, dry grass etc. in a jungle but everything would have been ineffective, scattered, disorganized, lacking continuity and uniformity. Can we imagine such a film now days?

In the beginning, films under the influence of theater and stage technology were overloaded with music and dialogues. Only one microphone fixed at one place, was used to record the dialogues. Similarly the camera was also kept at a fixed spot as it was difficult to move the camera at various places. Actors used to speak their dialogues, sing and dance in front of the camera. After one shot another shot was taken similarly. There were some limitations which were there in the nestling stages of silent cinema when a scene was photographed in a single shot. It was difficult to fragment the scene in various shots like Pudovkin and Griffith.

In India, fiction cinema came in to existence with Dada Saheb Phalke's 'Raja Harish Chandra in the year 1913. The films at that time were influenced by theater techniques. The way back ground music and sound effects in a stage play were provided live, silent films on the screen too were accompanied by live performances of musicians who provided music on a live orchestra from the front of the screen synchronizing with the visuals to make the scene interesting and enjoyable. The Speed of the films was also less than 24 frames /second as it was standardized later. This resulted in every action moving faster than its natural pace. The speed of a projector was also not standardized therefore there was variation in the shooting and projection speeds. This is very evident in those films which can be seen today.

Film- Raja Harish Chandra:

The Back ground music is played live on the harmonium.

1. L.S. Palace-King Harish Chandra, his wife and son remove their ornaments to renounce.
2. Exterior of the Palace- Harish chandra and his family come out of the Palace and climb down the stairs. People pay their respect by touching their feet. A saint asks everyone to make way for them

This scene of Raja Harish Chandra had been finished in just two static shots. Since it was the time when cinematic technology and editing was in its adolescent age so every action was mostly filmed in a single shot. Joining of two shots was necessitated for continuity of the story. The live music and effects supported the emotional contents. When the sound was introduced in cinema the back ground music and effects were recorded and synchronized for historical preservation of these films, that's why we find all the films made during silent era with recorded music as during the screening of these films now neither there is a provision and facilities for live performances nor it is desirable when recording technique is available today.

Initially people were astounded with the sounds for its novelty however soon they were disillusioned. The directors forgot that continuous sounds including dialogues take away the feeling of reality and experiences of a normal life which they had enjoyed in silent films. Few believed that the dialogues had not helped a scene tremendously. In a silent movie we see a dog barking; with sound we can hear him barking which could look real but not more than this. It does not increase the impact of visual expressions; it is still a dog barking. Similarly the dialogues in a scene also express the same as that of the visual images. When a dialogue 'get out 'is added with the visual images of an angry father pointing to the door and asks his son to go out, still has the same expression. In this situation the shot without a dialogue has better emotional appeal.' This may be true when the sounds or dialogues are used thoughtlessly however I think that discretionary use of appropriate sounds enhances the dramatic effect of a scene. We may not receive any additional information from the sound of dog barking but the sound definitely gives a feeling of reality. In the same manner whatever happens around us, its actual sounds add reality to the ambience effectively. We can judge the impact of sounds in a scene when we comparatively watch the same scene with or without sounds. Therefore it is unnecessary to compare silent and sound cinema. In silent movies actors' merit, facial expressions and communication were emphasized; in sound films dialogue adds to his acting capabilities and expressions when he can modulate his dialogues to convey inherent emotions of the scene to make it more effective. . The dialogues spoken in various tones and styles can produce different meanings and emotional effect if they are properly used by the director.

The introduction of dialogues and actual sounds brought significant changes in the narratives of cinema. The actors' characterization, performance and expressions are eased by the dialogues to give the audience an illusion of reality. Director too gets some more creative freedom to create and divide scene considering the dramatic effect of the story. Dialogues play an important role in transition of shots/scenes unlike use of a caption earlier. The dialogues can facilitate certain expressions just in one shot while in silent movies, the director had to devote many unnecessary shots and waste time therefore the dialogues bring down the cost of the film without compromising in the effectiveness of the scenes as the director can always use his discretion to have a dialogue or not. A location in the film can be established just in one word while in silent movies one had to use a visual image or a title/caption every time for the same purpose. Similarly a dialogue can pass on information in few words which was difficult if not impossible in silent cinema.

The dialogues in cinema have brought two important revolutions in film making such as; Variations in the story telling and higher standards in cinematic presentation. The film makers of silent era worked for perfection in story narration by resorting to indirect suggestions and symbols to impress their viewers by using over expressive visuals, different types of transitions and cutting of shots, use of symbols etc. while impact of sound films is instant and direct which is close to our normal life experiences. In sound films visuals and sounds are complementary to each other while undoubtedly a visual image has better emotional appeal therefore a Director has to be careful while working on a scene. It is very common to see a photo post card like visual images but they lack emotional impact on their viewers. It is due to technological advancements, special lighting and knowledge of cameramen that they work very hard to bring photo perfection to show beautiful visual images including fascinating locations without understanding the emotional requirements of a scene or a story. This is one of the main reasons for films failing at the box office. Therefore visual and emotional appeal of the story should never be ignored while shooting or editing a film. In Editing, generally editors make a mistake of fast cutting the scenes for fast pacing ignoring the emotional aspects of the story as every emotion has its own inherent pace, it should be presented without disturbing the same.

The basic principles of editing innovated in the silent era are equally important today as they were at that time. Close shots, Flash back, Dissolve, Pan Shot, Tracking and crane shots are very common today. They are the need of every director who cannot do without them; he can only change their execution for his creative interpretation but their utility to achieve maximum dramatic usefulness has not diminished. It may not be improper to say that these fundamental principles are still considered to be the basic grammar of cinema and no film can be made by ignoring them.

Sound and other technological developments have resulted in many significant transformations in the methodology of film making like determining pace of a film. It is not dependent on 'cutting rate' unlike in silent era. It can now be achieved through the volume and the control of sound tracks. Earlier 'passage of time' was informed by inserting a 'subtitle' which can now be done by a simple expression of a dialogue. The background of landscape through a moving train can now be created by 'Back projection' or other digital devices.

Sound has also affected the methods of editing. Special effects of silent era are outdated now such as 'Iris shots' being used earlier to draw attention are no more considered to be practical and real due to its artificial pictorial effect. Griffith's 'Masking shots' look completely unnatural. Similarly his 'quick or momentary flash back' used in his film' The Birth of a Nation' now look forced or implanted unnecessarily but few film makers still use them for visual variety however they must be required in the scene otherwise their use only for 'technical reasons' may rob the realistic flow. Another difference between the Editing procedures of silent and sound films is that of a 'form'. In silent movies It was imperative to show everything in 'Visual form' but with sound, Dialogues can convey the message in short and quickly. This can be understood by study of a scene from Griffith's 'Birth of a Nation'-

Shot 1. Mother assures her son who is lying injured on a hospital bed that she would take him to meet the President Lincoln.

Shot 2. Lincoln is seen in his study.

Shot 3. Caption.

Shot 4. Back to shot 1, Hospital.

In silent movies such insertion of captions were necessary to explain the audience about their conversations but in sound films such insertions are not required as dialogues can clearly and effectively explain about the content of conversation.

There are four main differences in editing of silent and sound films-

- The order of the shots. (Chronology)
- Selection of camera set up / angles.
- Timing.
- Presentation, flow or smoothness.

The Chronology of shots:

There was only one person working as a director and editor in silent films. Director then had more creative freedom because his objective was to attain maximum physical and visual continuity by most satisfactory chronology of shots. He used to shoot as much material as was possible and subsequently come to cutting table for shaping the film as per the script. Griffith practiced this method of shooting maximum and cutting on the editing table to achieve the best results out of what he conceived. For such directors it is said that their films are made on editing table. Eisenstein use to work on the details prior to shoots while his writing the scenes but the final shape to film was given only during the editing when he organized, arranged and juxtaposed his shots. German film makers are known to work on a perfect screenplay with all the details including that of sounds and accordingly edit their films therefore every Director has its own working methods and systems. Some are well organized and some others take creative freedom during the screenplay writing and execute their ideas during and after shooting to get the results as close as possible to their concept in the script. Their screen play works as their guiding document. When they are on location, they let loose their creativity and take full liberty with their imagination and innovation. Editor too has to be more creative and imaginative to edit such material. Most of the big directors and big production houses that produce high budget films with top star cast come in this category. They ensure that nothing should be left to chance during the shooting to repent later during the editing of the film. In contrast, Directors making low budget film are more précised in their concept and planning right from the script writing to the editing of the film.

Some people believe that sound films provide fewer opportunities to an editor to display his creative merits and imagination in comparison to silent films due to their liberty to juxtapose the shots as they liked. Physical continuity was not a major factor in such films to that of storytelling and emotions. Dialogues are a vehicle to carry forward the content and emotions in a sound film from one scene after another till the story culminates with a climax. Experimental and decorative scenes are added in the screenplay only with reference and context of the story in which Dialogues join one scene with another. Therefore it is always advisable to have a near perfect screen play including all the visual and audio details with scene properly and suitably conjoined. If the screen play displays full form of the film it is always easier for director and editor to shoot and edit later with more precision. Therefore it will not be wrong to say that the editing plan should be duly prepared at the time of writing by the writer and the director. A well conceived screen play gives a definite direction of the film to the Director that saves him from shooting unnecessary scenes and other ornamental material which directly affects the budget and expenditure on the film. Editorial planning during the writing of the script is much more important and required in low budget films. In this editorial planning, Director and

Editor together work on the details of chronological order of the scenes, transitions from one scene to another, details of shot taking, flash back or flash forward, Montage and development of the scenes etc. if there is a requirement of some special visual and special sound effects, they should also be mentioned in the screenplay. A detailed editorial planning does not restrict a director to his basic script or   stems his creativity but it gives him more clarity to improve on his script and incorporate new ideas in already planned out screenplay.

By this time we all have understood that shooting of a film does not commence in chronological order of the script. All the scenes in a location or a set or in a particular lighting arrangement or of an important artist as available are shot at a time. There is no similarity in the order of shooting the scenes and in the order of the scenes in the script.

The Clap Board :

To identify the shots in the script a 'clap Board' is used before taking a shot in an indoor or outdoor locations. After camera and recorder start rolling an assistant director responsible for exposing the 'clap board' displays and speaks written information about the scene on it in front of the camera. For a dialogue scene after recording this information, he 'claps' by the wooden board to record the 'clap sound' which is matched with the 'clap in the shot' for the synchronization later.. Thereafter Director orders 'Action' and the 'Take' of the shot begins with actors performing their act, camera moving, recorders recording the dialogues etc..

The Clap Board

The take ends when the director says 'Cut' after he is fully satisfied with the performance of every department in the take otherwise continues with further takes   till the Director and everybody else is satisfied. This shot is called 'O.K.' rests are called 'N.Gs' however many times an N.G take may not be a waste or a rejected one, it could be used partially or when a shot is to be repeated later as a reminder. The clap board keeps on track of the details about the take numbers, NGs or OKs. Another assistant also keeps a record of the details of the shots/ takes in '**continuity sheet',** we will discuss about the continuity sheet later.

The material which an Editor receives for editing is called the '

Rush' which comes in separate rolls of celluloid positive stock after the negative raw stock is developed and printed.. (Now a day the rushes are stored in digital data). These rushes are again not in the similar chronological order of the script. Not only scenes are scattered but also split and mixed with other rolls containing different scenes shot in the same schedule, therefore the first job of the Editor begins with the 'sorting' of shots and scenes with the help of information like scene no., shot no., take no. date of shooting and remark regarding OKs/NGs takes etc. written on 'Clap Board'. Where the strips of the clap meet with other that is the 'clap point' which is marked on both the visual and sound strips of the film. On the sound track clap sound is marked. This is required for parallel synchronization of the picture and sound tracks. Once the claps are marked, Editor synchronizes the picture and dialogues of each OK shot with lip- movements and simultaneously arranges the scenes /shots without removing any unwanted or extra length in the OK takes however NG shots are separately preserved and indexed for future. This step is called 'assembly of the rushes'. This assembly is the chronology of scenes as decided in the script or one can say that this assembly is the lose form of the film as envisaged. In other words 'Assembly of shots' can also be called as 'Lining up the shots' chronologically as per the actions in the scenes.

The camera placement and angles:

Commonly taken Long shots, Mid Shots and Close Shots in films are based on Griffith's principles propounded more than a century back. Most of the writers while writing the screen play suggest such shots in their scenes. Even if it is done by the

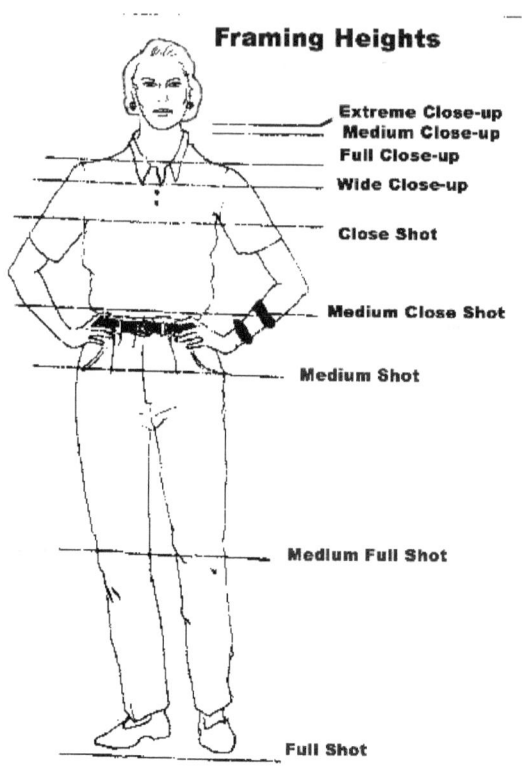

Framing Heights

Extreme Close-up
Medium Close-up
Full Close-up

Wide Close-up

Close Shot

Medium Close Shot

Medium Shot

Medium Full Shot

Full Shot

Sketch 1: Framing Heights

writers, it is the director who finally decides about the magnification or composition of a shot which includes position of the camera placement, angles and camera movements like tracking, tilting, panning etc. The writers during the writing stage can only presume the camera positions and angles etc however things may change drastically when on the set or a location his suggestions may not be practical and workable, Director has to step in for shot division once a location or a set is finalized. It does not mean that a writer should not give any suggestions on this issue. His ideas should always be respected as he works on the mood of a scene where he may feel that by a particular camera placement, movement or angle the scene would be more meaningful and effective. This also gives an insight to the Director to understand the depth of the scene. There have been instances that many writers worked on the script so methodically and minutely with details that their script was considered to be 'Ready to shoot' product. This helps new Directors who work with a professional and experienced writer however a Director can not absolve himself of his creative responsibilities.

Shots Type:

It has been a general practice for long since the inception of cinema to establish a location in Long shots, a character, person or an actor in mid shots, for detailed and minute expressions of an actor, his behavior, an object etc. in Close Shots as a fundamental rule. The distance between the camera and the object or character defines the Long, mid and Close shots. There can be ample variations in each category of shots by changing the distance between the camera and the object such as:

- **Long shot-**   Extreme Long shot, Long Shot, Medium Long shot,
- **Medium Shot-**   Medium Long shot, Medium Shot, medium close shot.
- **Close shot-**   Extreme close shot, close shot, Medium close shot.

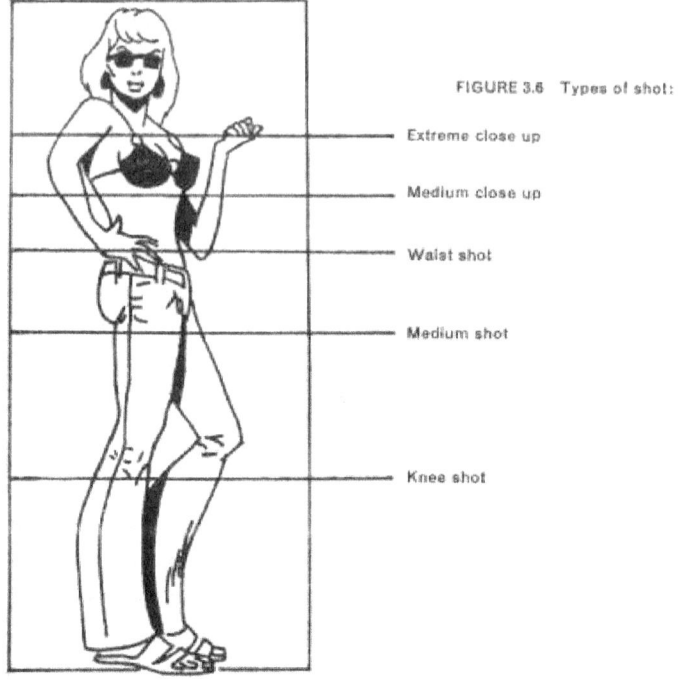

FIGURE 3.6 Types of shot:

—————— Extreme close up

—————— Medium close up

—————— Waist shot

—————— Medium shot

—————— Knee shot

Sketch 2: Type of shots

There is no parameter or a fixed measurement of distance between the object and the camera to decide about the magnification of the shots. It entirely depends on the discretion of the Director to place his camera and the object as per his concept and requirement of the scene similarly camera can also be placed in Low angles or top angles. The distance between camera and object and its angle leave different impact on the audience and the director must know it before he steps out for shooting. Shot division is also done keeping this factor in mind so the Director can shoot and Editor can edit accordingly. If the Director does not know how a shot would be juxtaposed with another on editing table, he will not be able to prove his directorial maturity and technical excellence and he may fail miserable in his execution of shooting and editing.

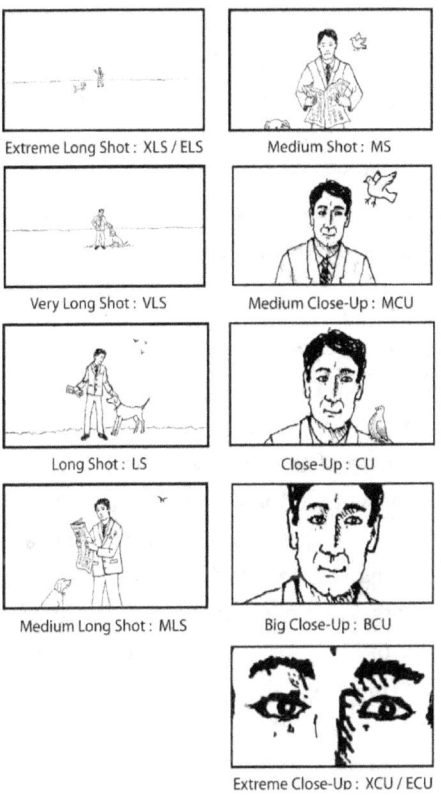

Sketch 3- Magnification of the shots

Timing:

When we talk of 'Timing' with reference to a film or a scene, it means the duration of the shot seen on the screen in the context of film speed with which the film runs through a camera or a projector. There is standard speed of 24 frames/second for celluloid film and for digital data it is 25 frames/second. All the machines and tools are universally geared up in this speed including editing and sound recording equipments. If they don't run on this standard speed, it will be impossible to have visual and sound synchronized. In editing this speed can be varied for functional reasons.

During the editing of silent movies, the length of the shots used to be reduced (Fast cutting) to establish 'tension' in the scene. It meant that the screen time for a shot was shortened. Similarly to establish thought process, loneliness or laziness of a character length of the shots were increased (slow cutting). This increased the time for a shot to remain on screen longer. During the chase sequences, climax or other action scenes, fast cross cutting was resorted to as a general practice by all the film makers. The timing of the shots is determined as per the character of the scene and the visual content. Sometimes a beautifully conceived and composed shot may not fit in to the character and pace of the scene wasting the hard work put in by the entire unit.

In sound films too there is no rule for screen timing of a shot. Editor is bound by the duration of the dialogues spoken by the characters in the scene. He has to follow the timing of dialogues spoken by an artist but he can still change the pace and emotional effect of the scene and the screen time of a shot by inserting reactions of other characters, overlapping of dialogues, insertions and cutaway shots, intercutting, showing parallel actions etc. he can extend the screen time by extending the length of the shots for slowing an action or for fastening the action reduce it by cutting short the shots. By parallel actions Editor can show a point or a counter point to increase the impact of the scene. Some time some symbolic sounds and visuals are used for a better effect of the scene therefore it is necessary to have preplanned editing of such things in advance of the shooting to facilitate the director to take such extra shots.

Presentation:

Presentation of a film is the illusion of life like experiences by the audience in which they live with the characters of the story. The way we experience daily events and happenings in our life without feeling a jerk or disruption, the way some times we are happy or sad, excited or irritated with our surroundings, things in life go on flawless, similarly audience become one with the characters on the screen, The transition from one shot to another and from one scene to another has to be flawless and smooth. It is wrong to presume that any shot even if it is the shortest one of only few frames on the screen can pass out of our eyes without notice and cognition. If there is no continuity in transition of a shot, we feel a sudden jerk or a heavy blow the way when we unmindfully step into a bump or a pit when walking smoothly. It will be difficult for the audience to come out of this sudden shock immediately. By the time they come out of it and start re-concentrating on the story, they will have missed out some very important events or emotions that kept them glued to their seats. The moving images on the screen are a series of still photographs which give us real life experiences when they run at a certain speed in the projector. Any disruption, disconnection or jerk in this flow irritates viewers until and unless it is the demand of a scene and the director had planned this way. This can be easily experienced by any of us if we see disconnected moving pictures. Some times Editor makes use of such jerky transitions to draw an attention to the technique without realizing that such gimmicks not only hinder the flow but also distract audience's attention therefore an Editor must never play with the visual and audio continuity for any reasons.

The responsibility to arrange shots in the chronological order, selection of camera positions and angles, timing and presentation etc. does not rest on the shoulders of an editor only but is equally shared by the writer, the director, the cameramen and the editor. Other departments extend their technical support to achieve the objective however with the advent of sound in cinema Editor has many more challenges to resolve any technical complications cropping up during the editing process therefore an Editor must be well off with the technical knowledge and foresee its implications in post shooting phases.

An example:

In the children's room Chiku and Mini play with toys. Camera on a crane moves from them to show elegantly designed and decorated drawing room of the house and tilts up to top angle to include friends Nilofer and Rashmi sitting and talking across a Glass table kept in the center decorated with Juices, fruits, dry fruits and other eatables. Nilofer holds the glass of juice while Rashmi offers her to eat something in between. Nilofer keeps the glass on the table and picks up some dry fruits.

Nilofer- 'Don't you want to know how I am here in your town?'

Rashmi- 'Yes, of course. I was surprised to see you in the market. (She laughs) Tell me what brought you here?'

Nilofer- 'I am here with my husband Nasir.'

Rashmi- 'Nasir... your husband? (She can't believe) If I remember it correctly, you were married to Kamran.'

Nilofer- 'Yes indeed then he went to Mumbai with his father to handle his recruitment business.'

Rashmi- 'But how come you are with Nasir and not with Kamran?'

Nilofer- 'Kamran and I are divorced and it is my second marriage with Nasir Hassan Mirza.'

Rashmi- (shocked) 'Just a minute....just a minute. Is he not the same Mirza who was mad for you?'

Nilofer- 'Yes, he is the same one.'

Rashmi- 'and he used to clash with Aamir.'

Rashmi's telephone rings. She moves to pick up the call. It was her husband Aamir on other side.

Aamir- 'Darling, There is some important meeting in the evening so I will be late today. Take care of yourself.'

Rashmi. 'I will take care of myself but what about you? You are going to miss something which you will regret for long time'. (Rashmi teases him)

Aamir-   'why do you say so.?'

Rashmi-   'It is a surprise. Now You decide if you want to miss your surprise or your meeting. Ok Bye.'

Rashmi returns back to her friend laughing. Nilofer looks at her curiously. Rashmi sits back in her place.

Nilofer-   'What about you? How is your husband?'

Rashmi-   'He is a nice guy. See him for yourself. Now tell me about your life. How is it?'

Nilofer-   'It is long story …'

Cut to-

Nilofer's Flash Back)

It is a common format for a screenplay which most of the writers follow. In the opening of the scene the writer has conceived a crane shot which he feels would be a good beginning introducing the location and main characters. The writer has also attempted to create some curiosity in the conversation of two college friends Rashmi and Nilofer about their marriage who are meeting after many years and they are not aware of what went on in other's life. While talking to her husband on telephone Rashmi creates some element of curiosity for him hinting to the audience that there is something which will be revealed later. The writer also tried to indicate some reactions of the characters during their conversation which Director may consider during the shoot and for Editor a placement for the reaction shots. Once the basic structure of the script is ready Director should work on the editing pattern in the scenes while doing the shot division.

It is important for a writer and a director to plan out the editing of the film during writing of the script itself but it may not always be perfect and practical to have a foolproof editing plan at this stage though it is a very important but in this preliminary stage of film making they can only roughly presume camera placements and angles, shot division of the scenes etc,. Locations and sets can be completely different when they are designed and finalized which can alter actors' moods and movements to a great extent during their performance but a writer should never shy away suggesting these things in his script to guide the Director and Editor subsequently. When Director is actually engaged in shooting, he should work on other technical details including shot division and editing pattern keeping the final shape of the film in mind. So once again it is reiterated that it is not the sole responsibility of an Editor but also of the writer and the Director to plan the final shape of the film with in the set principles of continuity, flow, rhythm and pace of the film however on the editing table it is the Editor who is responsible to execute and achieve the preconceived idea of the film technically. The conflict and the controversy as to who should claim the credit for editing of a film , writer, director or an editor will always continue but everyone should understand that film making is a 'team work' and no individual can claim the entire credit for a good or bad film. It is true that if a film is 'good' everyone in the film shares the credit but if the film is 'bad' it is the director who is failed in his vision, imagination, creativity and his leadership.

A controversy:

The veteran film maker of Indian cinema Yash Chopra once said,' I liked the story of 'Deewaar'. When writers Salim -Javed came to narrate the story to me, they had the hard bound script of the film that contained detailed treatment of every scene from beginning to end written very minutely. Every dialogue, transition of shots and scenes, detailed editorial plan etc. was perfectly worked out in such a way that the role of the Director was completely marginalized. It was a complete script in all respect. It was a deviation from the general practice of writing only a sketch script by others. It was perhaps the best script written till date by any writer.' Yash chopra, who not only created a niche for himself but was widely respected in the industry, 'Deewaar' is one of his most successful films in the history of Indian cinema. Salim- Javed is known as the most successful writers' duo of their time. They not only brought recognition for film writers but also earned them money and respect otherwise they were known to be a meek, tunic and trouser clad, unshaven and sickly persons who walked with a hanging knapsack and snapping slippers. Salim-Javed uplifted the writers to star status. Film writers became 'star makers'. Their remuneration was not less than a star actor. It was Salim -Javed who gave an identity of 'Angry young man' to Amitabh Bachchan who became a rage thereafter. The success of 'Deewar' was attributed to the writer duo and their script. If a writer can   visualize a complete film minutely in his screenplay, it robs the Director and Editor of their importance.

An experienced and successful Director would prefer to take all the decisions from selection of the story to the shooting and editing of the film but if a Director lacks the sense of continuity, shooting and editing techniques and technology, the entire burden of editing falls on Editor's shoulders. Every production house has its own production set up that includes a writing department where a team of writers work in tandem on the story, screenplay and dialogues etc. few others pick up a director first and then proceed to appoint writers and other technicians. In some studios from the writer to the director, actors and technicians are engaged on monthly remuneration and they work on their assigned task. Studio system was more prevalent in silent era but gradually it had been replaced by individual production houses however in television industry, such system has made a comeback where many are paid either on monthly salary or on payment per episode basis.

In United Kingdom, a Director is the most important person in the film production who supervises the writing and editing of the film to ensure a smooth flow of the film. In Hollywood, writers write screenplay extensively and the Director is expected to translate the same on to the screen. In this system role of a Director and an Editor is significantly reduced. In America producers enforce their authority in the creative and business matters including monitoring of the editing'. They don't consider it Director's responsibility where he is restricted to execute the shooting as per the written script. In some cases Director is not even given a script beforehand. They are only required to translate the screenplay in to a film. That's why most of the successful Directors prefer to write their own script. Sometimes they are the Producers of their own film too.

Whatever people may think about the role of a Director but there is no conflict about his supremacy in film making anywhere in the world. A Director is always a 'Director' who heads the entire team and the team has to work with him to realize his vision of the film. He is a link and an inspiration between various departments and execution of various technical activities, creative crew and the artistes etc. therefore the responsibility for the film's quality and success lies on him. Others are responsible only for their restricted performance, the success and failure of the film does not effect as much as it affects a Director. So any debate regarding the role and importance of any other department vis-a vis the Director is pointless.

Many Producers of big budget films force the Director and the Editor unnecessarily to keep the close shots of main actors to draw attention of the masses and fan following of the star. It is not a good practice as it effects the overall quality and impacts of the film because such shots or scenes are not only not required in the script but are avoidable. They are forced and hinder the rhythm and pace of the film. This distraction is felt severely by the viewers although they may not be able to specifically define it. If an Editor is bound to carry out the wishes of a Producer, there is still he can do a lot to avoid any visual distraction or discrepancy arising out by the frequent use of the close shots of the main actors by using intercuts, inserts and other ambience shots, and sounds etc. Without disturbing the mood of the scenes. These extra shots have to be taken by the Director during the shooting. It will be appropriate it Editor is able to discuss about extra shots in the scenes before hand or if he can personally be present at the time of shooting and keep his eyes and ears open to guide the

Director on the location. It may not be possible for the Director to deviate from the script and concentrate on these extra shots, Editor can do this job as he does not have any other engagement on the set.

*****

The knowledge of mechanical procedure for editing a film is important but not sufficient enough to become an Editor. . Every genre has a different style of editing which an Editor should know. Otherwise an Editor will fail in his objective and film will fail in its purpose.

CUT-3

Film Editing: The technique

Before we discuss about the methods and techniques of Editing it is important to know about the various procedures that are involved in its operative process which comparatively are much simpler than that of cinematography and sound recording.

Basic Editing Procedures:

Since the advent of cinema in the world film making has witnessed tremendous growth in the methods, machines, tools and technology. In the silent era films were shot on 'Film strips'. When sound came 'optical sound track' followed by 'Magnetic tapes' were used for recording the sounds. During the Editing of a film many types of tracks are prepared separately like Dialogue track, Effect track, Music Track, Incidental sound effects track, general sound effect track etc. It may be noted that during the shooting whatever dialogues are recorded, they are used to Lip- synchronize with the picture. This dialogue track thus, is called 'Pilot track' or 'Guide track' which is used as a guide for 'Dubbing' and synchronizing the same with the visuals. Once the 'final cut' of the film is completed and dubbing track is prepared, Pilot Track is kept aside and is not used for any purpose. These various types of track were then mixed or Re-recorded on the magnetic tape and transferred on the sound Negative for preparing final sound negative which is used along with the final Picture Negative for making the final print of the film. This final print is called 'Married print' because both the final picture and sound are printed on a single stripe of 'Positive film'. The same print is then sent to the cinema hall for screening through a projector so it is also called a 'Release Print'. From the shooting to the release of a film all the procedures were conducted on celluloid film but now the development has brought 'Digital Technology' in which everything from shooting to recording and editing is done on 'Digital Format'. Majority of cinema halls have also been converted to Digital projection system but still many single screen theatres are in operation where celluloid print is projected on a projector. While the Digital technology has proved to be very cost effective and less time consuming, the reasons for its gaining popularity, the International standards still consider celluloid is the best in quality and longevity, that's why many producers still prefer to shoot and release their films on celluloid format however the producers of small budget films consider digital technology a boon in film making that gives them an opportunity to experiment with the subjects and the genre,

Similarly there have been many significant development and changes in the 'operational procedures' of film Editing. Most of the films produced today are edited on 'Digital format' due to its cost effectiveness and the time saving systems. If the film is shot on celluloid, after the shooting is completed, the exposed visual and sound material is transferred to digital format by the process of 'Telecine'. After the editing is completed and film is finalized, once again the final picture and sound are transferred back on the film negative (picture negative and sound negative separately) by 'Reverse Telecine'. Thereafter both picture and sound negatives after parallel synchronization are sent for making final print or Married print in the film laboratory.

In the context of editing it is pertinent to note that in whatever format shooting is done whether is digital format for Television series, news coverage, Documentaries, events or reality recordings etc. or in celluloid format for commercial purpose, the basic editing operational procedures remain the same and are common to both formats. The difference is only in the equipments, machines and tools used for the purpose therefore it is more important to discuss the basic Principles of Editing primarily in the celluloid (film) format which has been the back bone of cinema and witnessed gradual and steady growth in cinema technology including Editing. Technology may change but not the basic principles.

Shooting:

After writing the screen play the next destination of a Director is to proceed for shooting. It should be understood that no shooting is possible or commenced in the same chronological order of the scenes as they are written in the script because every scene has different locations, sets and setting requirements etc. It is also possible that many more scenes can be shot in the surrounding locations but all those scenes may not come in the story in the same order. If it is presumed that shooting has to be done in chronological order of the script, than the Director will be visiting the same locations again and again till all the scenes in that setting are completed. Every time he visits the location or a set, all the preparations of the settings including the erection of sets, dates and permissions for shooting on locations and artistes, junior artistes, travelling, boarding and lodging of the unit etc. again and again will entail huge expenditure repeatedly. This could be conveniently avoided if the shooting is completed as per locations and sets. This saves a lot of production time, expenditure and manpower. Therefore it is always advisable to complete the scenes earmarked for a location or a set.

Picture and sound (Dialogues, incidental and general sound effects) are recorded separately during the shooting. The visuals are cinematographed by a camera and the sounds are recorded on a sound recorder on the same speed i.e. 24 frames /second in celluloid format and 25 frames/second in Digital format.. If camera and sound don't run in the same speed, it will not be possible to get the parallel synchronization of dialogues and incidental effects. When the post shooting work like editing and recording is taken up in the digital form before finally transferring back to the celluloid, one should always remember the speed difference in both the formats as it is to be followed meticulously while converting from one format to another at any stage, A difference of even a single frame will play havoc during the editing of the film.

Synchronization:

Some times while watching a film or a television serial we must have noticed that the picture is either coming before the

Elements of Film Editing

sound or after it. This irritates everyone. In a cinema hall, people vent out their anger or irritation on the projectionist by shouting there. The projectionist in fact has nothing to do with the fiasco. Only sometimes due to some technical failure, this may happen in the theatre but in most of the cases it is due to mismatch (Non synchronization) of picture and sound in the print which could be due to carelessness in the laboratory where print has been made. In most of the cases, such prints are out rightly rejected by the laboratory or the Producers, if not, such prints are sent to the interiors , touring cinemas, small cities and towns where quality of a film is not a criteria.

To facilitate the synchronization of sound and picture, during the shooting an assistant comes in front of the camera with the details of the scene written on a wooden clap board, reads them out and clap before the action starts. This is to identify the shots and the corresponding dialogues/sounds by the Editor who sorts out the shots and their respective sounds from the mixed bags of film tins. Once Editor completes the sorting of picture and sounds for each scenes, his next step is to synchronize them by marking the meeting point of the clap in the picture and clap sound in the sound stripes. When these two 'matching points' are marked and placed in a synchronizer, parallel synchronization is achieved however the Editor must be vigilant of some speed variations which might have occurred during the shoot due to malfunctioning of the camera and recording equipments.. After this he continues with the same process for all the shots of all the scenes and keeps on joining them together in chronological order till the end of the film. The material which is now handy with the Editor is called 'assembled rush print' which include all OKs and selected NGs Shots in which all the shots are assembled in synch without significant cutting except throwing out the blanks, delayed actions, extra length before and after the action etc.

By this time everyone is aware that 'picture' and 'sound' are recorded separately during the shooting in a standard speed of 24 frames/second for the film and 25 frames/second in Digital format. When these picture and sound tracks are placed parallel on a synchronized, we get a perfect synch, of picture and sound. To match them perfectly, the 'Clap' of picture and sound is kept parallel on a synchronizer.

After the shooting, picture and sound are received in separate rolls. The first job of the editor is to match or synchronize them. In this process Editor has to sort out OKs and NGs of the same scenes split and spread over in different rolls and bring them together and match in the same order as in the rushes. Thereafter Editor and Director scan through all the rushes with synch, sounds and 'select' and 'Mark' OK takes of the shots or any other take of the similar shot if required and keep them in separate boxes with details of the scenes on the label. Once this selection process is completed, Editor joins together all the selected shots in the order of the scene as it is in the script. This is called 'Assembly' or 'Lining up' of the rushes. Now this assembled material is ready for editing as per the script.

Editing- Visuals:

Editing on celluloid format (now replaced by digital technology which is more cost effective and less time consuming) is done on machines (now extinct) called 'Moviola', 'Acmeola', 'Editola' and 'Steinbeck'. All these machines basically are 'Viewing Machines' on which Picture and sound tracks could be run separately or inter-locked together after they are threaded on picture and sound heads. Editor can run them forward and backward in the speed of his functional choice- slow, fast or normal speeds or stop it on a particular frame. Normally the machines are used to mark 'cutting or synch Points' on the stripes therefore Editor is free to stop it at any frame whenever he wants. The machines are also used for the purpose of parallel synchronizing picture and other sound tracks. The correctness of synchronization is ensured by watching the synchronized picture and sound simultaneously on the small screen of the machines. If Editor finds it ok then he puts a 'mark' on the film stripes. An assistant Editor cuts them on the 'marked frame' 'and joins them together one after another. This is done when the shooting of one or more scenes is completed. This first cut is ready for the preview of the Director and Editor. This is the time when Director may find some shortcomings in the scenes and decide to shoot some more shots before winding up from the same location. If the Director is not available for the preview for any reasons, his representative does the job. This is done to avoid any shortcomings in the shooting of a scene while the Director is still shooting on the same location or a set. So it is a day to day work of Editing department to sort out, synchronize and make the first cut of the scene while Director is still shooting. At this stage of 'First Cut' the length or duration of the shots is deliberately kept longer because the scenes will require to be shifted many times during the course of editing and with every shift and editing some frames will be lost in cutting therefore some extra margin in the length of the shots is necessary. . In Digital editing no frame is lost as the entire material is stored in 'Digital data'. Anyway this is not the final stage of editing where one has to be very précised since the last word on the editing always comes in consultation with the Producer, Editor and Director. In between the 'rough cut' and the 'final cut' all the technical decisions like use of sound effects, optical effects (dissolve, fades, wipes etc.) are taken by the Editor. He decides about their place and duration.

Editing- sound:

The recordings including dialogues recorded at the time of shooting have many drawbacks like external noise, inaudibility, corrupt audio etc. that damage the sound quality significantly. Actors too concentrate more on their facial expressions and acting skills then their dialogue delivery during the shoot but still dialogues are recorded to be audible only for the purpose of editing. The Recordist is also aware that these dialogues are not going to be used finally except for editing that's why this dialogue track is called' Pilot track' or 'Guide track'. Now there are techniques available to record dialogues or effects on the location eliminating external noise where dubbing is not required. In this case the actors, director and the recordist have to be very careful and précised fully aware of the fact that they would not have an opportunity to further improve the quality of sound later, indeed a difficult task.

After the 'rough cut 'of the film is ready, the Director with the help of Editor and Recordist records the dialogues by the actors again in the studio. This process is called 'Dubbing'. The Dubbing is also done for other language versions of a film. These dubbed dialogues are once again synchronized by the Editor thereafter the Pilot track is kept aside. Once all the dubbed dialogues are matched, the Recordist works out the requirements of 'sound effects' in consultation with the editor. The sound effects include 'Incidental effects that are part of the activities or the incidents during the shot like footsteps, door opening etc. and other 'Environmental effects' that constitute the ambience of the scene. These effects are either recorded in the studio or location or pre- recorded by others. Now a days sound effects are also generated by electronic devices.

There enters the Music director who in consultation with the Director and Editor decides about the back ground music score and records it as required by the Director. The back ground music is not to be filled from beginning to end but should be sparingly used to create moods and emotional effects in the scene. If the back ground music is used as a filler to fill the silent gaps, it not only becomes monotonous but also jarring as audience doesn't get any respite which becomes irritating. Sometimes even 'silence' is more effective than the sounds therefore Editor and Director should not shy away using 'silence' often. The Music director while working on the back ground score must first get in to the soul of the scenes and take a decision accordingly. Otherwise he will face a danger of his music being completely out of synch with the moods and emotions of the scene. So scoring back ground music is a serious task and should never be taken casually to fill the tracks.

After recording of sound effects and back ground score the tracks are handed over to the Editor who proceeds with synchronizing them with the scenes in separate tracks such as Dialogue track, incidental sound effect track, general sound effect track, songs or dance performance track, back ground music track. The blank spaces in sounds are filled up with the 'silent sound track (SST). There can be more than one track in each type to facilitate the Editor to give guide 'markings' for mixing or re- recording. The 'Markings' provide the Recordist sufficient clues in the form of specific 'symbols' on the picture for proper 'fade in' and 'fade out 'of the sounds. Editor also prepares a dope sheet with all the information in chronological order for Re-recording to help Recordist in the mixing process. At the time of Re-recording sitting by the side of the Recordist, Editor keeps on telling him about forth coming sounds in the scene as per his dope sheet.

Re-recording or Mixing:

When the final editing is completed and all the tracks including Dialogues, sound effects and music tracks are laid and Editor has given prescribed markings, the scene shifts to the recording studio where Recordist watches the film with all the tracks separately on a special recorder that is called 'Mixer'. In the mixer Recordist first mixes individual sounds like dialogues, effects and music laid in more than one tracks into a single track in each type of sounds. This reduces the total number of tracks to one combined track of each type of sound. This process is called 'Premixing' of sounds when all the different type of sounds are mixed in to one specified sound track, For example, all the dialogues will be premixed on a single track from the earlier more than one tracks. Similarly all the effects spread in different tracks will be brought in to one. Accordingly music which included songs, dances and back ground music are also mixed in one track. This makes it clear that after premixing we have only one comprehended track of each of the sounds. These premixed tracks are now ready for the 'final mixing'.

In Re-recording first step is to mix all the tracks i.e. sound effects and music, except the dialogue track. This mixed track consisting of Music and sound effects is called 'International track'. The International track is required to dub the film in other national or international languages as and when required as there is no change in effects and music in other languages.. Releasing films in various languages including foreign languages has now become a very profitable proposition for Producers all over the world. Sometimes films earn more money in foreign markets and are also appreciated in international film festivals however the first priority of the Producers always remains with native market. Once International track is prepared the dialogue track is mixed thus we get the 'Final sound track' of the film. This final sound track is then transferred to 'optical sound negative' for making final prints. This process is called 'optical transfer'.

Negative Cutting:

Simultaneously on other side the 'Negative cutter' starts cutting picture negative as per the finally edited picture positive (Rush print). One can notice 'key numbers' printed on the left side of the negative stripes. The same numbers are also printed or replicated on the positive rush print'. The negative cutter parallel matches these numbers on the negative and the positive on the synchronizer and continues to cut and join the negative with reference to the positive print. It is also possible that some times 'Key numbers' are missing or not visible making it difficult to match them with positive. In this situation, a prominent action on the negative is marked and matched the same with the positive rush. Similarly on the sound negative, in case of missing or invisible key numbers, sound is matched with optical sound modulations which are clearly visible. Sometimes these modulations are also scrambled when one or more sounds are recorded simultaneously making it difficult to identify specific sound modulations. In such cases, modulations are read on a 'sound reader' to identify any specific sound for marking and matching. When this is done, Sound negative and positive can be matched easily. It may be noted that negative cutting is a very crucial and important stage one has to be very careful about it. Even a slightest carelessness and mistake may result in mismatch of action in the visuals or non- synch in the audio which is immediately noticed by anyone. Any mistake or wrong cutting of negative may result in permanent damage which may be difficult to rectify as negative frames are permanently lost. The final picture and sound negative of each reel are then matched parallel on the synchronizer and given 'Synch Marks' for the guidance of the laboratory technician who places them parallel on the printing Machine.

The Final Print:

The Cameraman and the Laboratory technician sit together and correct the tones and the colors on '**Color Analyzer'**. They analyze the colors and tones in each shot very minutely from beginning to end and carry out '**color corrections'** till the end of the film. The color correction at this stage is required because at the time of preparing the 'rush print' no color corrections and tonal analysis is done by the cameraman. After the color correction is completed, the first 'final print' is prepared. This first print is called the '**Answer print'**. This 'answer Print' is used for the purpose of Film certification, promotional trails and previews, further corrections in picture or sound quality if noticed by the cameraman or the Director or by any other technician in the answer print, can be carried out in subsequent prints for release otherwise the print is as good as the final film in its content.

The knowledge of mechanical procedure for editing a film is important but not sufficient enough to become an Editor. Mechanical activities in the editing process are generally carried out by editing assistants under the supervision of the Editor therefore assistants cannot be held responsible for any flaw and deficiency in film editing. It is the Editor who is accountable for his merits. An Editor before accepting the task must know the styles in editing different type of scenes such as, dialogue scenes, action, comedy, music and its performances like songs and dances etc. and various genre of cinema such as Documentary, advertisement, News and reviews, educational and instructional film, compilation etc. Every genre has its own specific requirements and purposes which should be reflected in the film and Editor must be aware of them. Every genre has a different style of editing which an Editor should know. Otherwise an Editor will fail in his objective and film will fail in its purpose.

*****

The complete action in a scene is fragmented in many shots containing partial actions. These shots are then joined together to form the entire action look in physical and mental continuity as one act. .

CUT- 4

Principles of Film Editing

The moving pictures on the screen create an illusion of reality in our mind. The visual action that is not real looks like a reality. The same realism takes us to establish an emotional bond with the actors playing a character in the story and we too become a part of them. We laugh when a character laughs, we get emotional when a character cries, and we are romantic when we see the hero romancing with a beautiful blonde. We love the hero and hate the actor playing a negative role. The way we are influenced by events in our real life, we are also affected by the happenings on screen. It is the sacrosanct role of an Editor to recreate the maximum realism by his '**cuts**'. If the scene lacks on this count, it is the failure of the Editor.

'In one evening I came out to my balcony to have a glimpse of the happenings outside. Saw few men beating another man. There were onlookers standing around in a circle to see the drama. No one tried to mediate and stop the quarrel. I could not stop my curiosity to know the reasons of this assault and came out of my house immediately, stepped down from the stares. Before I could know the reasons and mediate, everyone started scattering when they heard the sound of police siren. I remained there. The man, who was beaten, was handed over to the police. The victim later told the police that he was a picketer and was running away after his act when he was caught by few persons and beaten up. Police took him in the van and left. I continued looking at the van going away and returned home after some time.'

On my back home I continued to think about the incident for some time, in normal course anybody would have forgotten about it but I could not. I did not know why I felt some sympathy for the boy. I could feel the helplessness on his face when he was surrounded by people and was beaten up till the police came to rescue him. I remembered seeing people living and sleeping on the pavements, I also remembered beggars on the traffic signals. I saw young women squeezing milk from their dried up glands to feed their new born. I have seen poverty in its crudest form so I was sure that the boy was not a criminal but became one out of his hunger. Similar emotions take over our feelings when we watch a film and live with the characters on the screen.

Assault of a picketer :

1. **M.S., Evening, Interior, The room   with the Balcony.**
   The character comes out from the room And stands in the balcony looking out on The road

2. **Top angle shot, actor's view point, Exterior, Road.**
    Down below on the road few persons are beating another man.   Onlookers   stand around to see   the   drama

3. **Close shot of the character**
    Character is curious to know more about the assault.   He   turns   to   go   down.

4. **Long shot, Interior, building's stare case.**
    The character opens the door and comes down on   the   stares.

5. **Long shot, Exterior, Road.**
    The character reaches to the place of incident

6. **Mid long shot, Exterior, actor's view point, Road**
    Assault on the man is continued. People around him are watching and enjoying the action.

7. **Close up of a boy gesticulating. Exterior.**
    A boy in the crowd is instigating people to beat him more. The sound of police siren is heard approaching near

8. **Mid shot, Exterior, Road**
    People turn to the direction of the siren. The character too looks to that side.

9. **Long shot, Exterior, Road**
    The crowds disperse here and there. The

character stays on.

10. **Close shot of the actor.**
The character looks at the police van and then turns   to   assaulters.

11. **Long shot, Exterior, Police van and   policemen.**

12. The police van stops near the place of event. Policemen try to stop the quarrel and arrest the victim.   Assaulters   stand   quietly.

13. **Mid shot, Exterior, Police and the picketer with other people**
A policeman enquires. One of the assaulters informs him that the man is a picketer and was running away after pick pocketing when he was caught   by   people.

14. **Close shot, Exterior, Picketer.**
The picketer is frightened and crying for another beating. He begs to be excused with folded hands.

15. **Mid long shot, policeman and Picketer**
 Policeman pushes him in to the police van

16. **Close shot, Exterior, Actor.**
Actor looks at the police taking the picketer in to the van.

17. Long shot, Exterior, Road.

Police van is seen going away.

As an observer It is normal to be attracted instantly when such events take place in our life and our mind starts comprehending various actions of the events by carrying out automatic 'cuts' and ' joints' to establish ' unity' of different actions. Thus we automatically keep on psychologically editing various routine activities of importance. Our mind accepts only those things which are important and related to an event while other unimportant and insignificant activities in the surrounding like traffic jam, movement of vehicles, vendors selling on roadside, people walking on footpath are negated and ignored. Above example can be understood from the perspective of an observer but in films a camera acts like an 'observer' which captures any event in long shot, mid shot or a close shot considering the importance of various actions. These shots are used by the Editor to create an 'actual effect' in the scene. If the above scene is shot from a camera, the edited scene *would be somewhat like the following:

In the above scene there are two perspectives which are clearly observed- one is entirely from the point of view to the main character as a straight line experience in our daily routine. These straight line experiences occur the way our eyes see them where there is no opportunity to analyze things minutely. We see the objects in a single or fixed focus but when the same scene is shot through a camera we have the liberty to choose the focal length and the distance between the object and the camera in number of shots which are subsequently arranged in proper order, place and time to create a psychological reflection of reality. The Editor could have easily shown the complete scene in a single long and view point shot of the character (shot no. 2) where the actor is standing and looking at the happenings on the road as we see in our life but a close up was necessary to establish his curiosity that prompts him to go down to the place of quarrel therefore as in shot no. 4, he opens the door and comes on the stare to go down. If this shot is not used it would be impossible to show the character reaching to the spot. His jump from balcony to the road will not only be unnatural but will be disconnected. It would give a mental jerk to the audience therefore shot no. 4 is very important for the physical and mental continuity of action. When the actor reaches to the spot of quarrel, it is imperative to show the assault action in closer perspective (shot no.6) to satisfy the curiosity of the actor as well of the viewers. The shot no. 7 reflects the general reaction of the people around represented by a boy who is instigating people to beat him more. The moment they hear the approaching sound of police siren they start dispersing slowly but the actor continues to stand there (shot no.9).The sound of the siren takes the scene forward as the actor (also the viewers) wants to know the reason of the quarrel. The moment police are informed that the man is a picketer, he is frightened for another beating and cries begging for excuse (shot no.13) but the police takes him into their van. In the scene the audience is not given an opportunity to be judgmental, it is the Editor who tries to psychologically engage people by using   various shots which give them the necessary description of the event dramatically. It would be impractical to expect the audience to draw their own inferences and feelings about the event if they are shown the scene in a single long shot, it would be very ineffective and monotonous that's why it is the Editor who has to recreate and psychological reality of an incident from beginning to end of the scene by using proper shots in proper place and proper time. For this reason only the principles of editing and the editor gain credence and importance in proper shaping of the film.

During the era of silent cinema a very simple plot was presented to touch the emotions of the viewers and the Director was compelled to use many unnecessary shots and scenes including 'Title cards' to convey his ideas. In fact the use of captions in between the film was an obstructive necessity for the uninterrupted narration of the film. The use of sound in the film made story telling easy but there were many other financial and technical challenges a producer had because making a sound film incurred more cost than making of a silent film. It was a daunting task for a Producer to arrange this extra money as no financier was ready to finance an artistic or an emotional film just for creative satisfaction of a Director since the financer wanted to recover his investment in a film. For this purpose the film had to be commercially successful. During the hundred years of the existence of cinema, this situation has remained unchanged and a Producer still faces the same challenges when he makes a film. The commercialism and the business considerations have overtaken film production all over the world. Producers started experimenting with the tastes and choices of cine goers by incorporating elements that draw them to the ticket windows of a cinema hall. It was also not commercially and technically necessary to narrate and edit the film in a simple and straight manner with the use of dialogues. It is possible only when actors develop their movements and dialogues taking care of the continuity in their physical actions. It is an uphill task for a Director and Editor where there is no 'direct continuity' and the scene required 'Juxtapositions' for its development. Sometimes in such a situation use of sound is also not normal and routine as in the following example:

1. "(Camera is outside). A man is walking on a corridor of a Hotel .we hear his footsteps. He moves towards a door and tries to open it. We hear the sound of lock being opened. After unlocking the lock he opens the door. (The shot is cut in the middle of door opening)

2. (Camera is inside). The door opening from inside is matched with the movement of door from outside in the earlier shot. The man comes in and closes the door. .

   There is another Character in the room and we hear their conversation."

In this scene both the characters are established before they start talking and their dialogues in close shots are cut alternatively. Some times wherever it is necessary, their reactions in close ups are inserted in between their dialogues. In reaction shots, few words of the dialogues of other character are overlapped. This is an example of a simple and straight narration where pre decided action and dialogue continuity is maintained. In such type of editing, one shot is cut as soon as the dialogue is completed. There cannot be a pause in a continuous flow of conversation. Reaction shots wherever needed are inserted/overlapped in between the dialogue of another actor. In such scenes, there is no problem in the use of incidental sounds even if the pace of the scene is more.

In the following example the physical continuity in editing is absent. A sequence is constructed after mixing many unrelated and disconnected scenes.

- An instrumentalist is reaching to crescendo while playing in a concert in a hall.
- The chief guest, who is a Prince, is sitting in a box.
- A revolutionary is fixing the fuse of a bomb beneath the box.
- The beloved of the Prince is arriving in a cab.
- Close shots of the player in crescendo,,
- the Prince enjoying the instrument,
- sparking in the fuse,
- Prince's beloved arriving in the cab. The pace of the scene in increased by shortening the length of the shots."

In this example the eyes have identified the instrumentalist, the prince, sparking in the fuse, Prince's girl friend. All these shots are no where physically connected with each other but when they are juxtaposed, they produce a visual and thematic continuity. In the climax, fast cutting and the short length of the shots including few frames of a fraction of a second too does not take any visual out of sight. If we see these visuals with the actual sounds they produce, it is noticed that the length of the sounds is much more than the length of the visuals. If we cut the sounds as per the length of the visuals there will be lot of confusion. The scene will not only be ineffective visually but sound also be jarring with abrupt sound cuts. While few frames of a visual are enough to create a desired effect, we may have to provide more space to the sound to be noticed. Similarly while we can create a visual unity by creative editing without their actual sounds, the same audio-graphic unity will not be felt without visuals. The length of the shots can be reduced gradually to increase tempo of the scene when approaching the climax which is not possible with individual sounds. In sound, it is practical and advisable to use a single sound to the climax. It can be achieved by increasing the rhythm in the musical instruments or by any other sound instruments where variations are possible according to the tempo of the scene. Incidental sounds can be used in between to create realistic effects.

Dialogue scenes:

In the editing of dialogue scenes it is possible to cut the shots of two or more talking characters alternatively so that they can hear and understand others' view point. Such view point shots (VP) in a dialogue sequence are generally taken from 'over the shoulders' (OS) of one person who stands opposite to the talker. In such cutting of shots Editor induces actions and reactions of the talking characters to create dramatic effects and carry forward the emotions of the characters to the viewers. It may not be possible if the entire conversation is shown in one combined shot. View point shots connect audience with their on screen characters emotionally that's why when a Director narrates a story on the screen it is not just his one man view point or experience , it is the view point of everyone including the audience who is part of the scene. It is the reason that a viewer experiences multidimensional emotions while watching a film. To create such multidimensional emotions a Director takes shots from various angles, distances and perspectives which are arranged in proper order, place and time according to the script by an

Editor to the best of his creative merits however it is the Director's prerogative to give or not to give importance to any part of the scene. It is decided by the Director in his creative wisdom before the commencement of the shooting and accordingly he composes the shots to create a physical semblance. Although a viewer may not live his personal life the way on screen characters live but would always like to experience it in the same way as it is on the screen therefore the audience accept the Director's creative freedom in the dramatic presentation of his characters. Sometimes similar liberty is taken by the Editor when he cuts a shot abruptly to create a dramatic effect. By doing this he takes shelter of the principle of 'sudden attention grabbing' in our life to continue with the psychological continuity. It is like our common experience when we walk on a road sunk in deep thought process and suddenly disturbed by a continuous honking of a car that stops in front of us, we are saved of an accident. We come out of our thoughts, look at the car, pause for a while to compose and move ahead. In the editorial design, a character is crossing the road mechanically unconscious of his surroundings when a car honks and stops near him. The character returns back to his senses and looks at the car. He pauses to compose and slowly moves ahead. In this scene stopping of the car with a loud honk will be an 'abrupt cut' because it is part of the scene so the viewer will mentally accepts it conveniently. Sometimes such 'abrupt cuts' are made to enhance the dramatic effect of the scene. An Editor therefore should be given some liberty to display his creativity when cutting a shot until and unless a Director has some suggestions. This is his contribution like an actor in the film.

Continuity:

What continuity in cinema means and what is its significance..? Normally cinematic continuity is regarded in terms of physical actions and proper timing of actions and dialogue delivery. While physical continuity reflects a sense of continuous physical action, the continuity in dialogues means proper timing in their delivery. The dialogue should flow consistently with 'natural' pauses wherever necessary as we do in real life. More and less pauses may be a hindrance in proper communication of the idea.

An Editor has two methods in his command to create continuity. First he assembles all the shots as per the chronological order of the scenes and makes a 'rough cut' in which shots are kept with some extra length than required. In 'rough cut'. The form of complete film becomes clear. Thereafter the Editor watches the film many times to understand the dramatic and emotional requirement of each scene. It is also discussed with the Director, if he has any specific suggestion about a particular scene or editing pattern. Once the ground is laid with proper consultation and understanding of the requirements, the Editor begins smoothening the scene by removing unwanted and extra length and frames of the shots by proper matching of actions and suitably reducing or increasing the pauses in between the dialogues to avoid any noticeable jerk in actions and the dialogue to let the audience have a free flow of the scene without jerks..For example, a boy is walking on a road in one shot and in another he is eating on a dining table. These are two different disconnected actions, joining them together will not be acceptable as they lack action continuity and a visual illusion. Therefore some mechanical principles have to be followed for 'smooth cutting'. These principles will be explained in the forthcoming paragraphs however sometimes an Editor may deviate from these principles for creating a dramatic effect at his discretion.

Action Matching:

It is necessary to achieve flawless continuity by properly matching two actions of consecutive shots of the same scene. If a character gets up from his chair to get chilled water from his refrigerator, in the next shot he should be shown moving towards the refrigerator and in the third shot he should open the door of the fridge and complete the action. This is called 'action continuity' but if the character is sitting in one shot and in another he opens the door of the fridge, he will be jumping the action without out reference of his prospective action. Such a cut will flout the rules of physical continuity however there are provisions for resorting to 'Jump cuts' to reduce the 'action time' but these 'jump cuts' should never be abrupt and jerky. They have to follow the principles of physical and psychological continuity to give the audience an illusion of reality.

We all know by now that the complete action in a scene is fragmented in many shots containing partial actions. These shots are then joined together to form the entire action look in physical and mental continuity as one act. . Many times the same action is shot from various camera angles and distances. In this exercise the continuity of the back ground is very essential therefore one has to be careful to maintain the same background in each shot so that it does not look like happening in a different place in similar action. For example if there is fire in the background of the scene, the same should be shown in other shots where action is taking place at   the same time. The properties shown in the scene should not be disturbed and form the same background for the shots. The 'continuity' of everything is a prime concern for creating unity of visuals whether it is costumes, properties, set and settings, lighting arrangements, dialogues, actors' 'looks' or the main action etc. It is not necessary that all the scenes are shot together at a time but still the continuity as mentioned above has to be maintained. For example- there are three shots of an action of a character in his black suit –He leaves his home, sits in his car and reaches to his office. All these shots may not have been taken at a time on in a single day but the character should always be seen wearing his black suit in all the three shots of this scene. It is also possible that there is a long gap in shooting of these shots therefore one may forget the design and the color of the suit and it could be a big continuity lapse if it is changed and not taken care of because one cannot imagine and accept the change of clothes in one continuous action. Editor too will find it difficult to edit such a scene and rectify the blunder. Similarly care should be taken to maintain other types of continuity in the shots.

Due to staggered shooting schedules and disconnect in chronological shooting, it is a difficult task to remember and maintain continuity' of various nature until and unless a perfect record is maintained which can be referred any time during the production of the film. During shooting all these records of continuity are maintained by an Assistant director in a sheet that is called' **Continuity sheet'** or a 'Dope sheet' as some people call it. The 'continuity sheets' are the reference material for assistants in direction and camera departments in future shootings if required. It gives details of the shots, distance and angles of the shots, actors' movements, NGs and OKs shots, number of takes dates and locations etc. The continuity descriptions are recorded in triplicate, one is kept by the continuity assistant for his verifications and continuity checks during the shooting, another copy is provided to the Editor for his reference and the last one is handed over to the Production Department of the company. The still photographer also keeps on clicking 'working stills' of each action and the set of the scene from various angles. These photographs serve the purpose of checking continuity of costumes, properties used in the shot, set design , settings, action, Looks to the camera , Direction of the actors' movement, lighting arrangements etc. These still are normally clicked before the shooting during the rehearsals and the preparation for next take. The still photographs are also used by Art director and assistant directors for reference when the set is to be reconstructed, redesigned or altered. 'Repeat actions' in the consecutive shots are taken to provide multiple 'Action matching points' or 'Points of cutting' to the editor to avoid action gaps.

A very common continuity lapse is that of 'looks' which means the direction where an actor looks when he is standing in front of another character in a dialogue scene. We all must have observed in the mirror that when we look to the 'left', our mirror image looks at the 'right'. similarly when a person 'A' stands opposite to another person 'B' in conversation ,like a mirror image his looks in the camera will be opposite to the person 'B'. In this situation the viewer becomes a character A or B and camera becomes his eyes and the character opposite to him becomes his mirror image. Therefore when in conversation A looks to the left of B, the person B will look to the right of A from each other's view point respectively. In the same manner they will look to the camera as if they are talking to another character. If both the actors look in the same Direction, it will look that another person is looking away. It will be a great physical and mental continuity jerk on the screen.

Another continuity lapse that should never be committed is that of the direction of actor's movement. If a person is passing from left to right of the frame in one shot, in the preceding shot he should continue to move from left to right. If he moves from right to left in the consecutive shot, it will give an impression that the actor is returning back for which no reference or cause of action has been established therefore it will be a continuity jerk and will not be acceptable. Similarly when two characters from opposite side approach each other, one should be moving from left to right and another from right to left. This will give an impression of their narrowing the gap. If both of them move in the same direction it would mean that they are moving separately to the same destination altering the entire meaning of the scene. If they continue to change their direction of the movements from left to right or right to left without reason or a cause of action i.e. to change the direction in different consecutive shots of the same scene, they will create more chaos and confusion in the scene and the audience will not be able to decide which direction the characters are heading. Wait.Wait..Wait... it does not mean that an Editor or a Director can never change the direction of movement of an Actor in a scene or a character is forced to move only in one direction. He can always do so provided the Director plans for it before the shooting and takes some more extra shots suggesting the change of direction. These extra shots can be used as 'cut away' or 'insert' shots in between when the change in movement is required. If for any reasons Director has not been able to take such 'cut ways' or 'inserts' during the shooting, an Editor may try to find out such shots from other similar scenes in the film or from the stock material from other films otherwise he can also use general shots of the location or ambience etc. with due care taken for proper visual or thematic continuity.

It is not more difficult for an Editor to execute action matching between two consecutive shots than to incorporate suggestions made by other people as to how and where a 'cut' is to be made. For example-,' A man is sitting on a chair and a glass of beer is kept on a table in front of him. He bends to pick up the glass from his right hand and sips.' A Director may shoot such a simple scene from various angles which provides multiple cutting alternatives. Sometimes these alternatives may leave people confused as there is no fixed formula for cutting a scene. Every one may have different opinion and everyone seems to be right. It is there that Director and Editor together may zero in on the best option.

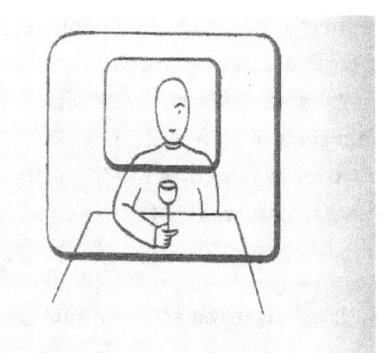

Sketch 4

Sketch 4: Three main angles- Close up, medium and long shot.

 In the above scene Editor has many choices to cut from long shot to the mid shot. He can start action in long shot and cut to mid shot at any point when the actor is seen his hand moving up or down.

- He can start with long shot and wait for the action of lifting his hand is completed then cut to mid shot to complete full action.
- He can start action in the mid shot till he touches the glass to his mouth and cut to long shot when he takes a sip and returns the glass back to the table. In between a close up of his sips can be used.
- Action can be started in close up. The moment he touches the glass to his mouth cut to long shot when he takes a sip and keeps the glass back on the table. After some time action can be repeated in mid shot.

It is noticed that there is no jerk in action matching in all these alternative methods of cutting as cuts have been made where there is a pause in the action. In the 4th option use of the actor's close up indicates his intention to pick up the glass therefore there is no gap in the mental process of the action. This also creates curiosity in the minds of the viewers about the next action so when he is shown the complete action in long or mid shot; it is easily understood by him. .' Repeat' of the action helps in extending the 'Filmic time' that could imply that the character is waiting for someone and is just killing his time.

- If we start the scene in mid shot and show entire action in close shot then we have to match action in such a way that the main action of the scene i.e., drinking is in close shot. Mid shot may continue till he lifts his hand cut to close up to give importance to the main action of the scene.

- In another option Editor can start the scene with close shot when he looks at the glass. Cut to mid shot. after some time he picks up the glass cut to long shot in the mid of action when he is picking up the glass and takes it to his mouth then again cut to close shot when he sips the liquid in matching action. When he moves his hand out, cut to mid shot again and continue till he keeps the glass back on the table.

An Editor has ample opportunities to display his creative merits by choosing the best cutting option out of many available to him. In the last option above, shots have been repeated by reducing the length to increase the pace of the action without disturbing it any way. Here it is also important for the Editor to ensure that the pace of the scene is compatible and similar to other similar type of scenes in the film. If some scene is slow while other is fast paced, it will be a ping pong like feeling which is not acceptable however pace is also decided by the inherent nature of the scene. In conflicts or action scenes the pace will be higher than the normal conversation scenes. Editor has two options to make a 'cut'. He can do so in the first place while the action has some static pause or a point and another in 'motion'. It is not at all difficult to cut a shot in static points but if it is cut in motion there can be a jerk due to variations in the speed of the action which is very normal during the shooting, it is possible in the above mentioned example as the three shots have been taken separately with some time lapse in between the shoots therefore actor may not be exactly able to match the speed of his actions. Variations may be visible when he lifts his hand to pick up the glass, takes it to his mouth and keeps it back on the table. In such situations Editor faces some restrictions in editing. It is also possible that due to wide difference in speed of action, he may not be able to use some shots then he has to settle down with the most suitable shot or he has to cut it on static points. Such decisions are taken by the editor only. Another caution an editor must take while cutting in motion is to see that whenever a cut is made in the motion, the movement should not be very short and in different speeds. It may give a jerk as the shot will not be registered properly due to its short length so here editor should opt for cutting on static points. If two shots differ widely in movement speed, joining them will give speed jerk so editor should cut the shot with movement of similar speed.

Contrast in Image size and angle

We see three shots of a man in sketch 5, one is a full shot and others are comparatively closer. If a cut is made between A and B, the cut will be insignificant and will give an irritating continuity jerk that will give a feeling of some frames missing from the shot. Beside it will not add anything dramatic and emotional in the shot. When a cut is made between A and C, it will not only be significant, noticeable and effective but also adds visual novelty and curiosity for the new revelations in the shot which takes the scene forward. A cut between A and C will be smooth and acceptable therefore an editor should always keep it mind that a cut between insignificant visual change either in size or angles will hinder the continuity and emotional flow without adding any dramatic and emotional effect in to the scene. The contrast between two consecutive shot should be significant, visible and noteworthy.

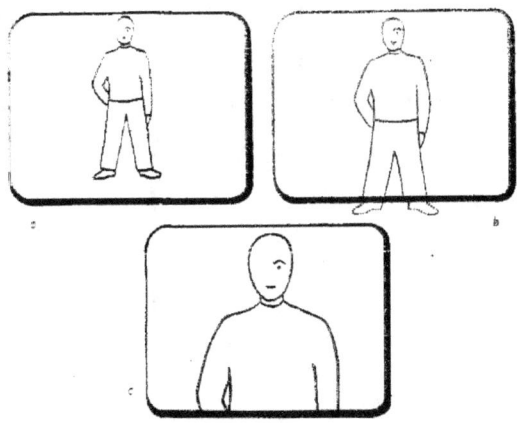

Sketch 5- There is insufficient contrast to make a smooth cut between a and b: A cut from a to c makes a distinct contrast.

Similarly in the following sketch 6 figures shown in the shots are almost similar so if a cut is made between A and C will be acceptable but not a cut between A and B which have no distinct variation in the size of the object which is clearly visible between A and C. It is clear from these examples that until and unless there is a visible contrast in the consecutive shots in size and distance, a cut should never be made. If at all editor has no option than to use the shot, he must use an 'insert' in between the similar shots to provide a distinct separation and avoid a continuity jerk. It should also be remembered that a cut should always be made to increase the dramatic and emotional effect and carry forward the scene to next action.

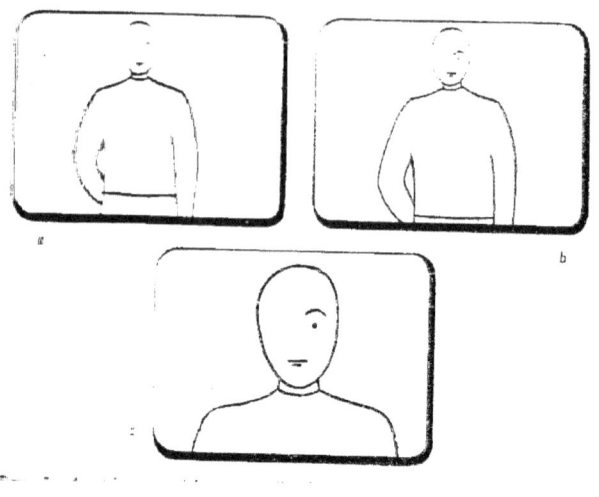

Sketch 6

Sketch 6 - A cut from A to B in too small a change in Image size, the cut needs to be   considerably closer as in C. Similarly the way we consider contrast in the size of the image we also have to make sure that shots in similar angles are not cut as this robs the concentration of the audience. Such cuts prove to be futile and ineffective. They don't serve any purpose too.

In the sketch 7, camera positions have been demonstrated to take medium and close shots. In the shot a character faces the camera in the back ground of a lamp post. First we cut from shot1 to 2a where lamp post is in the similar position as earlier this cut is acceptable as there is no change in the position of the man and the lamp post except that they have come closer. Opposite to this shot 2b also reveals the same with a little change in the angle that results in shift of the position of the lamp post. The viewers think that lamp post has changed its position on its own and came to the left of the man. In both the position the man remains static in the center of the frame but as per 2b lamp post has automatically changed its position which distracts audience's attention. This cut will also not be smoothing hence not acceptable.

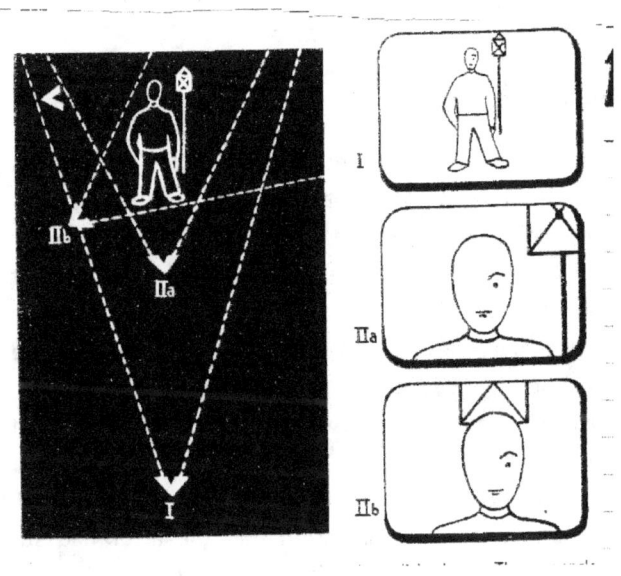

Sketch 7

Sketch: 7- 2a faces in the same direction as 1. 2b makes a slight change. The same angle or a marked change is to be preferred. During the shoot the problem could be solved by shifting the lamp post a little to the right of the camera. This would not change the position of the lamp post and would be in a similar position as in shot 1.

In any other situation if the editor decided to cut a close shot there should be a perceptible or marked change. If the camera is fixed in 90° then a cut from mid shot to close shot will be easily noticeable and there will be no jerk or a continuity issue. The character will be seen in profile instead of front therefore there is no need to maintain the same back ground because with the change of the angle, the back ground ought to be changed which is alright.

Sense of direction:

Eyes play a very important role in our body. It is the eyes through which we are not only seeing an object but also identify and recognize things for their characters, behavior and the types etc. we see their movement and distance, their position; left or right. In films this job is done by a camera, its lens works as our eyes. But there is a difference, when we see something, we see it from a fixed distance but camera can move anywhere near or distant, left or right, top and bottom, any angle or direction. If in one shot actor moves left to right of the camera, in opposite direction actor will move right to left direction giving impression that the actor had started moving in opposite direction. This is a visual jerk therefore actor should be moving in front of the camera in such a way that there is no interruption or diversion in natural course of his movement. If an actor is required to change the course of his motion from one direction to another, it should be properly established by showing the change to avoid confusion about the knowledge of direction.

In the   Sketch: 8- cuts from 1 to 2a and from 1 to 3a are clear, the cut from 1 to 2b would not be clear.

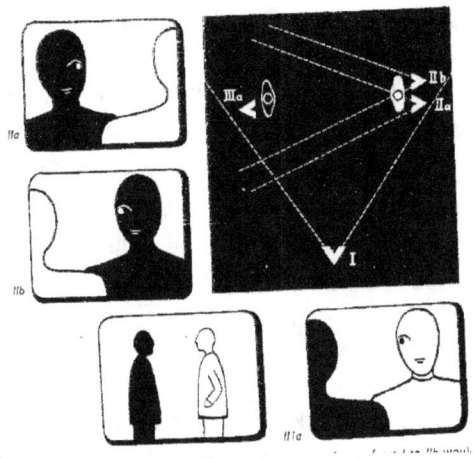

Sketch 8

In many war films we have observed that the armies of opposite parties move towards each other from two different directions either left or the right. Their entry in the frame becomes their identity and this identity of them is preserved throughout the scene. It means in every shot their entry will always be in the same direction which they have been given. This avoids confusion of their identity, movement and actions. Similar principle is applied to the characters in a scene. If two different characters are approaching each other from opposite direction, it becomes their identity in the minds of the audience. Confusion in direction occurs when close shots are to be used when they are in conversation with each other. This can be avoided by taking care of the looks of the character which should look natural on the screen. The direction of the looks should not change with the change of angles. In the above sketch an example of the use of close up is demonstrated. In the shot character A and B stand opposite to each other. The issue arises as where the camera should be placed to take a close up of any of them. In camera position 2a character B will look left to right as in medium shot so cut will be fine but from the view point of 2b character B will be seeing right to left which is not correct because the direction of looks of actor B will be suddenly opposite. The same is applied on A too therefore shot has to be taken as in position 3a. Characters are identified easily through 'over the shoulder-OS.' Shots. In close ups if shoulders are not visible their direction of looks in medium or close shots should be same.

Camera position is not as important for the determining the sense of direction as is to know how characters come in and go out of the frame but whatever direction they choose they must continue to move in the same.

 In Sketch 9, A cut from 1 to 2a maintains the same direction of view; a cut from 1 to 2b reverses it and is confusing. If a character moves out from the right of the frame and enters in the left of the frame, it will be a proper transition but if he enters from the right side of the frame it is wrong because the actor changes his direction by 180° without a reason or a purpose. If his change of direction is required in the story he should move as in sketch 10 below that shows his turn around then only viewers will accept it. By showing the turn around of the actor we mentally prepare the audience to see him moving in opposite direction and when the character starts moving in opposite direction, the audience normally accept it. It is like telling, a person has changed his mind and decides to return back. The rule is important for proper continuity of direction but can be deviated whenever there is a need to do it.

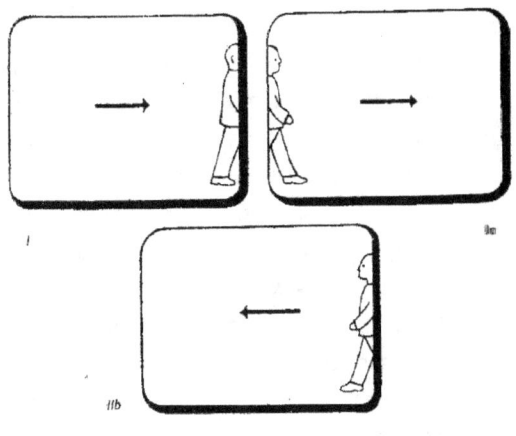

Sketch: 9

Sketch 10 (Below) - if the actor does reverse his direction, it should be shown as in b; a direct cut from a to c would be unacceptable.

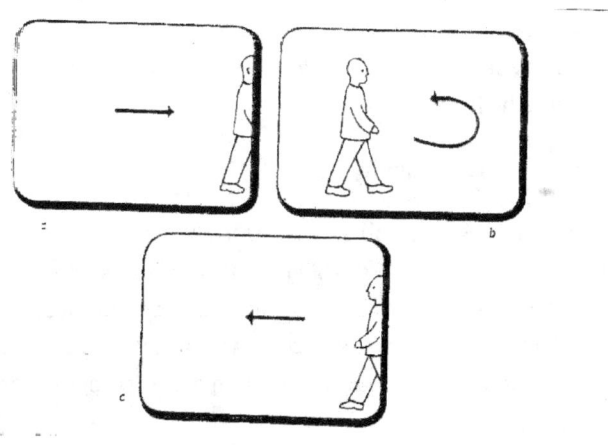

I would like to make it clear that there is no rule in film making that cannot be changed but it should be done with a reason and a purpose. These principles and rules are only guiding factors for a film maker. Editing is not a straight jacket procedure with many restrictions which cannot be over ruled. Right from the evolution of cinema, Editing too has evolved its own methods and procedures by trials and errors. Editors develop their own style and system to overcome any problem taken place during the shoots. They can break earlier conventions or they can formulate new rules and procedures but to do this they must know the ground rules of editing. In one of my editing assignments, I deviated from the established procedure of sorting of the material, assembly of the rushes, marking and cutting rough cut in this common order. What I did was little different but it saved lot of time on cutting table. After sorting of the material I did not go for assembly straight away but started marking, cutting and joining loose shots in chronological order so I was doing simultaneously marking, cutting and joining directly for making the 'Rough cut' of the material . It saved a significant time on cutting table otherwise if I had taken up the above work one after another in practiced chronology, it would have wasted more time so an editor can always devise his own methodology depending on the type of film genre he is editing.

Clear and Lucid continuity:

Normally a long shot is used to establish the location of the scene where events are going to take place subsequently thereafter other closer shots are taken but it is not necessary. Many film makers start their scene with a close shot because of their intention to create some drama and suspense; once they are successful in raising curiosity, they go ahead to establish the location of the event but establishing a location at any point of time during the scene is a must otherwise all the actions on the location will become meaningless without a reference. If there is a dramatic change after location is established and the scene shifts to another location, the new location should be established. It means that whenever there is a change in location, it should be established to take the audience to another location. Without it viewers will not be able to associate the actions with the locations. Establishment of the location is also important to establish the position of the characters and their movements.

Tone Matching:

During the shooting of a film the cinematographer tries to create visual effects by special lighting arrangements of the set in general and shots in particular. The lighting is a reflection of cameraman's creativity, vision and photographic quality. When these shots are cut Editor should also keep in mind that he does not make a cut between the contrasting lighting arrangements. If it is done viewers would immediately feel 'Tonal jerk' and it would called a 'harsh cut'. Editor must try to cut the shots with similar tonal effects. If due to some technical reasons it is not possible then the Editor should make a note of it and inform the cameraman to make necessary color correction at the time of printing.

Basically 'Tone matching' is the responsibility of the cameraman and the Art director but Editor must make an effort to not to cut shots of opposite color tones. Tone matching becomes difficult when the raw stock (picture negative) from different companies is used or when stock shots from different films shot earlier in different types of raw stock, different gauges, different color speed etc. are used. such problems crop up in low budget films or in documentary films, compilation films etc. where a film might have been shot by different cameramen in different lighting set ups and difference in individual lighting styles etc. such tonal differences create hurdles in continuity. Sometimes an Editor is compelled to make cuts that are mechanically not proper. It happens when the Director has not taken shots properly or which are technically wrong or when Editor has no other options, such cut cannot be avoided however the impact of the 'jerk' can be reduced by overlapping of sounds on other consecutive shot as audience attention would be diverted to the sound and the jerk will not be noticed severely.

Filmic Time and Distance:

The dramatic effect in editing means that no cut should be made if it does not contribute in dramatic, scenic, story narration or emotional purpose. However as we have repeatedly reminded that there is no rule in film making which cannot be changed but it should be done with a purpose.

'A character with a cigar in his mouth enters in to the room to search for a lighter. He looks around and finds the lighter on a center table. He moves forward and picks it up. He lights the cigar when he hears the sound of a door bell. He moves towards the door and opens it.'

.This scene can be picturised in more than one method.

 The scene can be shot just in two shots. First shot can be when the character enters in to the room with a cigar in his mouth and searches for the lighter till he finds it on the center table. Second shot can start from the point he picks up the lighter to the opening of the door. In principle, this cut will not be wrong as the audience will be seeing the entire action continuously.

Two: Now let's see the effect if the same scene is shot and edited in the following manner-

1. Long shot-The character enters in to the room with a cigar in his mouth and looks around for the lighter.
2. Close shot-The light is kept on the centre table.
3. Mid shot-The character enters in to the frame after some time and picks up the lighter. He lights the cigar. The door bell rings.
4. Close shot of the character looking at the door.
5. Close shot of the closed door.
6. Close shot as in shot 4-He switches of the lighter and leaves the frame.
7. Mid long shot-He enters the frame and opens the door.

In comparison of both the style of editing it is observed that in the first one the action is matched in a simple cut when the actor picks up the lighter. There is nothing wrong and extra ordinary in the editing pattern as viewers are able to see the entire action from the actor entering in to the room till he opens the door. Audience's attention is in no way deviated as the entire scene is enacted in real time and the actor's movement is normal so the cut acceptable. Now let's come to the second pattern. In the first shot actor enters in the room and looks around for a lighter when in he finds in shot 2 that lighter is kept on a center table. In shot 3 M.S. after seeing the lighter for some time the actor enters in the frame and picks up the lighter. The viewers understand that by the time they looked at the lighter, the actor has covered the distance to come to the table. This way editor has reduced the distance and the timing of actual movement of the character between shot 1 and shot 4. In shot 4 while he is lighting the cigar he hears the door bell and he looks at the door. From his view point shot 5 L.S. of the closed door is shown. In shot 6 C.S... He switches off the lighter and moves out towards the door. In the consecutive shot 7 M.L.S. after showing the closed door for some time, actor enters in the frame and opens the door. Here also Editor has reduced the distance and the timing of the movement between the table and the door. The viewers understand that by the time they saw the door actor has covered the distance between the table and the door so they accept the cut without reservation as they too mentally covered the distance with the actor therefore the Editor has not only satisfied the psychological needs of the viewers but also reduced the filmic time and distance which is very important in a fiction film where the story of an entire life time has to be visually told. If the Editor does not reduce the filmic time, the story will be stretched to many hours therefore it is necessary to reduce the incidental time of actions. It can also be understood from the following example-

'A man comes out on the lobby of his 25th floor apartment, comes to the lift and Waits for it. When the lift comes and opens, the man gets in, lift moves down to the ground floor with stoppages in between to pick up others. Incidentally the lift is stuck up on the 20th floor.   After some time door opens and people come out of it. The man along with others descends on the staircase to the ground floor . He gets in to his chauffer driven car and moves to his office through busy roads and crossing many signals. His car stops in the lobby of a commercial building. He gets out and moves to the lift where many people are in cue. After some time he gets in to the lift and reaches to his office on the 5th floor. His staff stands up to greet him. The man enters in his chamber'

If this scene has to be shown in actual time and pace, it would have taken at least an hour to complete the action however by using the theory of filmic time the Editor can reduce the incidental time and distance by skipping unwanted or extended movements of the actor. The man comes out and catches the lift on his 25th floor. The lift goes down to 20th floor (stoppages in between 25th and 20th floor are skipped) the lift stuck up. We see some reactions of desperation of the people in the lift. The door opens people come out and walk down on the stair case. We cut to people coming on the ground floor (here the waking on staircase between 20th floor to first floor is skipped). The man gets in to his car and moves on the busy road and stops at a signal. Once the light turns green, the car moves again and reaches to the office building. (The long distance between residence and office is reduced drastically by just a suggestion of a signal showing heavy traffic on the road). The man comes out of his car and reaches to his office directly (his journey from the ground floor to the 5th floor is skipped.).It is observed in the scene that lot of unwanted actions and distances which don't contribute in the development of the scene have been reduced or deleted without compromising on the continuity and completeness of the action. Viewers are travelling along with the character without feeling anything missed. Editor shows the main action without retaining unnecessary physical actions and movements, intervals and gaps in the totality of actions.

In another example; character A and B are talking on a roadside. After some time A tells him that he has an appointment with his girl friend so he has to go. B accepts it. A's girlfriend is bypassing many lanes and by lanes and reaches to a garden where she waits for A.' in this example there are two location connected with A. In the first one he is talking to B and in the second one his girlfriend is waiting for him in the garden. These two locations are linked by A through his dialogues. Editor may travel with A after he leaves B, through lanes and by lanes to his girlfriend passing a long way. In other method, A tells B about his girl friend waiting in the garden. Editor cuts to a close shot of waiting girl friend when viewers will be aware of her anxiety caused in waiting and will also be psychologically prepared to shift to another location. A leaves B. in close shot B looks at A going away. In the next cut Editor shows A entering in to the garden. By doing this Editor reduces A's movement and travel distance to the minimum. Viewers travel through the distance and reach the garden with A without realizing the reduction of distance and time as they are psychologically prepared to shift and move with the character A. in such cutting one may notice a disconnect in the physical continuity but dramatic impact of the cutting compensate for the physical jumps.

Screen Duration:

Editor decides the pace of the scene or the entire film by reducing screen time by cutting interval in the action. It means that deleted action has been completed behind the screen. By reducing filmic time we take an action forward. It can also be done by reducing action in two consecutive shots and join them in such a way that action seems to be continuous. In this method the length of the shot is reduced and action is matched in such a way that nobody is able to notice any reduction in length. For example -A character is walking up to the stares. Camera is on his back to presume as the character reaches near to the stares he will be shown walking up in profile shot. These two shots should be cut in such a way from where the action can start. It is not necessary to cut when the character reaches to the stares to show that he is climbing. He could be walking few steps (remove the rest) and in the next shot after few steps he climbs up (remove the earlier length). In such cutting pattern action is reduced to the minimum without having a physical jerk in the visuals.

In shot 1 it is established that that the character is heading towards the staircase and in shot 2, he moves towards the stares from point 'x'. It means that cut should be made few steps prior to his reaching to the stares. This cut may not be physically correct but if no jump is felt by the viewers, it is acceptable. The idea of the character reaching and climbing on the stares makes the jump insignificant and people don't bother about it. Therefore the 'continuity of ideas' becomes more important than the mechanical smoothening which should be preferred in every juxtaposition. The new Editors joining the profession give more importance to the mechanical details of cutting by ignoring positive values of editing then the psychological or mental continuity. Mechanical continuity is not the end but a means to attain dramatic and purposeful effect in the film.

Timing:

The Editor and the Director manage filmic 'Timing' of an

incident or an event by reducing or increasing it. By cutting intervals, a gap in actions and leads before and after the action etc. Editor increases the speed in comparison to the real life happening. With this method Editor serves many positive purposes. Editor presents the scene in a new perspective and dramatization by reducing the intervals in actions and events. It depends on the Editor's creativity as to how he arranges the events in appropriate place appropriate space. Every event or action must be placed considering its maximum dramatic effect in the most appropriate time and space. This leads an editor cut a shot in proper 'Timing'.

Let's minutely observe the difference in intervals between our real life conversation and a filmic conversation to understand the proper timing of our actions and reactions. For example, if a man asks someone, 'where are you going? 'other person replies promptly,' I am going to Jaipur.' This is 'quick reaction', and then there will be an interval of few seconds. If a person slaps another man without a known reason, the other person would take some time to understand why he was slapped before he reacts. This is called' delayed reaction'. Thus in every scene Editor manages proper 'Timing' by reducing or increasing the intervals between actions and reactions in such a way that the viewers psychologically accept the intervals. Editor should be careful to decide that there should be proper and acceptable intervals between an action and a reaction. If the interval seems to ne abnormal and unnatural, the scene will become ineffective and disturb his attention. In comedy scenes 'quick reactions' are appreciated while in suspense 'delayed reaction' heightens the mystery. Editor must introduce a new element of a 'surprise' or 'shock'. This keeps the audience glued to the screen.

While editing a scene the Editor should always bring new information with an element of 'surprise' or 'shock'. It should not come as normal in narration but it should be preplanned in context with a scene in totality and be brought at a proper time for maximum dramatic effect. In suspense scenes Editor can warn the audience by informing them about the impending dangers to keep them on their toes. When the fear factor is reduced or eliminated completely and they are unsuspecting of any mishap, Editor can again bring the main point of danger, this 'shock' will be long lasting. There is always a dilemma for an Editor as to when he should induce the fear factor, shocks and surprises in the film which is difficult in comparison to a 'Climax' which comes as an inbuilt factor in the script and the Director works for it in the script prior to the shoots. Such dilemma normally occurs for the use of close ups. For example, a man fires at him in an attempt to suicide. If his close up is used before he fires himself, viewers will be anxious to know about the suspense. If close up is used while he shoots himself, it will be a 'surprise' for the audience. If a little interval is provided in between these two shots then it will create a sense of uncertainty among the viewers which will increase their anxiety about the next move of the character. The editor can thus create a sense of surprise, shock and anxiety by reducing or increasing the intervals in the action to create intense dramatic effect in the scene. It also depends on the creativity of the Editor as to how and when he would use a shot to create desired interest. Long shots should be retained for longer duration than the close shots because it takes longer to understand the content of the long shots.

Pace:

In fiction films chase scenes are very common and popular. No film is complete without a chase scene because they have the power to glue their viewers to the screen and an Editor has ample scope to play with the material available to him for a chase scene. these are the scenes where an Editor can really display his creativity if he understands the power of a single frame that can be used to create the desired effect of 'Tension' the foremost requirement in a chase scene.

The Editor has very important method at his command to create moments of tension by reducing or increasing 'screen duration' of a shot. This also decides the 'Rhythm' and 'Pace' of the scene. The purpose of such cutting is to create more screen romance by applying number of mechanical means. In this process the pace of various incidents are decided to create more stress, tension, anxiety and suspense. Managing Rhythm and pace helps in retaining viewers' interest in the scene. This can be done either by playing with the length of the shots to recreate its own rhythm and pace or by retaining the inherent interest of the scene as part of the story .it may happen that in spite of fast cutting, scene may remain ineffective and slow. It is evident in many chase sequences of fiction films where though edited fast, scenes are kept longer than required. It mostly happens due to lot of material shot for a scene and the Director and Action director want to keep as much as possible. They look at the scene individually and not in its totality with the film.

Sometimes scenes with a slow pace are more effective than the fast cut scenes as happens with 'emotional' and 'mystery' contents where viewers' involvement with the scene is more proactive. Proper music and sound effects also play an important role in increasing this effectiveness provided visuals are also dramatic and effective. superficially created speed if required in the story can create more interest however one should not ignore the content of the shots .it is not a good idea to cut a scene faster if the content requires emotionally slow movement or cutting a scene faster when action is already fast. Every shot has its own inherent pace and meaning that gives a feeling of fast or slow. So it is not necessary that every time pace of the scene is decided by reducing or increasing the length of the shots. Just to increase the pace Editor must not resort to fast cutting unnecessarily. Even if it is needed to fast cut the scene the length of the shots must be of such duration that viewers are able to register it properly. If the eyes do not register a shot, it does not deserve to be there. For example if a Director uses a caption with some written words in close shot, the length of it should be at least readable. If it is not then the shot does not serve its purpose for what it is used. It also implies that Director is trying to hide something. If the length is more than required it becomes boring and unwanted. Similarly entire movement of the character in the shot must be shown otherwise it will looks abrupt and incomplete however there could be more than one shot in the movement with action matched properly. No shot should be cut in between a movement just for the sake of increasing the pace. The static shot conveys more information in a short period but an action in long shot requires more duration for its registration.

Now a days creating artificial pace of the film is one of the main reasons for the failure of the films in box office as they are not able to physically or psychologically take their viewers on the journey of the characters of the story in normal time leaving them completely disconnected with them emotionally. An Editor must understand that a close up is effective in shorter length while a long shot takes some time to understand so he should keep it comparatively longer. The length of a shot is principally decided by its image size and not by the whims and fancies of the Director or the Editor. After discussing the content of a shot and the Image size, it is to be understood that whenever an information is passed on for the first time by a shot, its length should be little longer than the information which are already provided to the audience earlier. Just to keep the pace high one should not resort to fast cutting, if it is done then the entire film would be running in the same pace that would be monotonous and unnecessary boring after some time. The pace leading to climax is gradually increased and the pace of climax should never be repeated in the entire film otherwise climax may lose its impact with diminishing anxiety. Where two parallel actions take place in the same pace editor should continue to cut them faster so the viewers understand both the scenes in the minimum time without wait.

Rhythm:

The 'Rhythm' in a film is like 'rhythm in an orchestra sometimes slow, sometimes fast, sometimes heavy in musical connotations, sometimes ascending or sometimes descending, sometime steady and soothing. It is similar as in literary works where writing is punctuated by coma and full stops. The purpose of both is to maintain a continuous interest in the work of art. We know that every scene has its own pace and rhythm so the Editor must not interrupt in its normal course.

Editor should retain the original and inherent pace of a scene to let it be more effective. In this procedure the film will have 'punctuated pace' it is difficult to understand the difference between pace and rhythm in context with the length of the shots because the length of the shot largely depends on its content. The rhythm of the film can be understood only after watching a portion of the film. Inconsistent or jerky rhythm when forced on a scene can be easily felt. The rhythm based on sound and music can be created easily because of the inherent beats that create a rhythm. Earlier while discussing the cutting points we discussed that preference for cutting in static points must be given than cutting in movements. This retains the normal flow of an actor's performance and an editor does not interrupt in this natural flow. When the editor cuts in a movement, he disrupts in the natural rhythm. This artificially created rhythm disrupts the continuity. Similarly no cut should be made except for reaction shots, in the running dialogues. Dialogues should also be cut at a pause. The cuts in between a dialogue are like coma and full stops therefore a cut should be made only to serve the purpose of giving a pause or its completion. A cut anywhere will be like putting a coma or a full stop when it is not required. It is not technically and professionally proper to cut anywhere to increase the pace of the film. While shooting Director and Actors create a special rhythm, playing with this not only breaks the natural rhythm but also makes it irritatingly ineffective. Editor cannot serve any purpose by cutting few frames here and there but it exposes his lack of knowledge, aesthetic sense and professionalism.

An Example: 'In the evening at sunset there is a routine weekly market and fair in a village. Hawkers sell their small items in make shift shops and on the ground. Villagers are buying things of their needs and bargain with the sellers. Sellers try to attract and call people to their purchase points. Some film songs are played in the back ground and some joker is entertaining people at some other place. It is an ambience of happiness all around.

Suddenly one hears the sounds of horses' hoofs approaching near. People run helter skelter. There is a scene of stampede. A harbinger informs every one shouting,' The robbers have come. Escape everybody'. we see fear in close shots of the people. Hawkers and vendors pack up their belongings and try to hide them. Shoppers run away when the sound of bullets fired heard. The dacoits come near in the mid of intense stampede.'

In the first part of the scene we observe peace and pleasure in a weekly village fair which the Director has established in various activities. Long duration shots in the scene reflect the slow and calm life of a village. Villagers are leisurely buying and bargaining. If the Editor tries to increase the pace by reducing the duration of each shot, the scene will not only be ineffective but will not represent the rural milieu. The moment horses' hoofs are heard; villagers are scared and run here and there in speed. The Editor creates a fast pace by fast cutting of the shots to create the changed mood of fear and concern for their life. Camera too moves fast to follow people running away. Suddenly the slow paced scene becomes faster. We see fear on the faces of villagers in close shots. Vendors pack their belongings and try to hide them. The fast back ground music also contributes in this pace. The shots in the air are fired. Background music is suddenly silenced and short length of faces of shocked people in different actions is shown in freeze frames. The silence of the music increases the shock effect which makes the scene more effective. Approaching Horses' hoofs are overlapped on freeze frames. Then frames defreeze one by one. Dacoits come close and once again there is stampede.

In the above example timing of each action is emphasized. Sudden burst of fast paced action after initially slow one that takes place when the harbinger informs about robbers coming in to the village. The pace again sinks with the firing in the air. Back ground music stops and we see the shock on the faces of people in freeze frames exposing emotional vacuum. After some time with the arrival of dacoits action is fastened once again. The alternatively changing pace of the scene creates a special rhythm which is dramatic as well as emotional and natural. Considering the nature and the gravity of the situation from happy to scary no one can question the aptness of changing the pace frequently with the change of the situation. The freeze frames enhance the sense of shock and dramatic quotient. The Editor has brilliantly used various mechanical techniques to develop the scene naturally effective displaying his creativity and merits. The monotonous rhythm in long shots has suddenly been converted to fast pace by the use of close ups. In this artificially created rhythm emotional elements have been given priority which was absent in unedited rush print.

Juxtaposition:

It is not that one can decide the pace of a film by reducing or increasing the length of the shots but how they are juxtaposed. There are ways and means to have variety of transitions, it could be a 'direct cut' or through optically created special visual effects like Dissolve ,Fades (Fade in and Fade out), Wipes,etc. if there is an interval between the duration of consecutive events (time lapse) a dissolve should be used. In a dissolve one shot gradually fades out while other simultaneously emerges out of it. But it is not necessary that every interval has a dissolve. It can also be done by a suggestion in dialogues by making a 'dialogue cut'. Fade in and fade outs are also used to show a time lapse. In fades, a shot gradually darkens (fade out) and another brightens (fade in) on the screen. Unlike dissolve the shots in fades come in and go out independently one after another. Similar functions are for a wipe. As the word suggest a 'wipe' wipes out the first shot giving way to the next one simultaneously. Editor must carefully choose any of these options for juxtapositions as required. Sometimes even for a friction of a moment viewers may feel little disconnect during the transition and feel a continuity jerk. The duration of these transition devices is also an important factor. While deciding the duration of a dissolve, fade or a wipe editor must keep the entire pace of the scene in mind. A slow transition in a fast scene or a fast transition in a slow moving scene will be disastrous.

There is another alternative of joining two scenes together is a 'Flash back' in which Editor takes its viewers back in time to reveal the past events which have bearing in the present and in future incidents of the script. Dissolve in a flash back or a fade out may hamper the continuity of the film as in fades screen goes dark for some time. This blank space has no meaning or the purpose therefore until there is a purpose these devices may not be used. Sometimes dissolves are used to create some dramatic effect in which two or more images are superimposed like it is done in a 'montage'. Wherever some pause is required for some dramatic effect dissolves or fades can be used. The pause given by fade out and fade in prepares the audience to think about the next situation. Here fades can create a positive outcome.

Selection of shots:

The Editor receives huge amount of rushes which contain thousands of feet of visual stripes and hundreds of shots taken from different angles and distance in various sizes. Out of this material editor has to make a difficult choice of selecting the best and most appropriate shots to build up an effective scene that is dramatic too. Therefore the selection of the 'right' shot is the crux to make a scene effective. Director, actors and the cameraman perform their best to create a very effective scene but the burden of selecting a shot even from the NGs lies on the shoulders of an Editor. It is he who with his imagination and creative vision digs out the pearls from the ocean of film material which can derive the maximum dramatic and emotional results. He can also use the balance, unused, left over and extra shots for creating special effects. These special effects are normally not described in the script or thought of earlier. There is no formula for selecting the best shot but while doing so Editor should consider the inherent sentiments and meaning of the scene and prefer the shots accordingly. He should not select a shot which is technically superior but does not make a sense in the scene to be effective. Normally Directors insist to use such shots as they have invested a lot of money and creativity to shoot them. Sometimes it is the reason for conflict between a Director and Editor. In this situation Editor must resolve the issue amicably by demonstrating him with the results and convincing him to agree to his point of view. Situation becomes more difficult when the Director is also an Editor himself. I would like to share one of my own experiences in the similar situation I landed myself in.

I started my career in fiction films as an Editor after coming out of the premier film school 'Film Institute of India' but after few years of struggle I took up direction of documentary films against my choice. I was not cast for 'Pure documentaries' till then therefore my style in the documentary films was also highly influenced by the techniques of fiction film making from writing screenplay to the taking, editing and the use of sounds etc. In one of my Documentary films 'Red Palm' I along with my cameraman had taken a master shot of about one and a half minutes (Apr. 140 ft.).We invested a great deal of efforts and time to take this shot by using lights and shadows. There was a movement in every frame either of the camera or the object to ensure that the shot was not steady at any point of time. We used all sorts of tools like crane, trolley, pan and tilting camera operation which were very difficult. When the shot was completed to our satisfaction we all were very happy and excited as such shots were rare in a documentary film .The shot was a challenge for everybody as they were not geared and experienced for such camera operations. Technically I have always been the Editor of my films; the Editor assigned was mostly an operative person. When we sat on editing the film I told the Editor to assemble the film as per the script which was very precise, and make a rough cut. My 'favorite shot 'was also placed appropriately. When we watched the rough cut my Editor told me to remove this shot as it was not going well. I thought for some time but Editor was not wrong. Our unit's enthusiasm and heard work splashed in to my mind. Removal of the shot would disappoint everyone including me. Shot was so good that I was not prepared to sacrifice it easily. The Editor was keen to know my opinion on his suggestion. I was in a dilemma. After some time I said, 'I agree with you as an Editor and remove it but as a Director I would like to keep it.' He smiled on my reply but matter was serious and was to be decided at the earliest. There was a conflict between the the Director and Editor in me, at last Editor won. My favorite ' Master shot' was too slow comparatively to other shots and it was hindering the pace of the film so it was better to be dropped and it was unceremoniously buried in the waste bin. So an Editor without falling in love should select a shot which is cumulatively compatible to the pace and the rhythm, story and narrative of the film.

Editing sound:

'Principles of attention' normally decide when the visuals are selected in editing as 'when I am writing this book my entire attention is centered on my pen, diary, subject and the vocabulary. I don't see anything else like table clock, phone, book rack, ceiling fan, door etc because my concentration is on my writing. There is a knock on the door and my attention is diverted to the door. My daughter enters and leaves after doing her work. I again return back to my writing.' In this small scene my complete attention is on my writing initially when I do not see or hear anything which distracts me till I am disturbed by the knock. I look at the door and see my daughter enter and return after some time. I come back to my writing again. In this scene, it is observed that the attention is shifted many times and is distracted by some other things and we start seeing those things. Similarly in editing 'Attention' is created by cutting of shots. Whatever we want people to see and hear we cut to those visuals and sounds.

There are variety of sounds in our ambience and environments. If we are standing in our balcony and looking out we hear birds chirping, traffic sounds, music being played somewhere, Ghrrrrrrr of the washing machine, tick tock of the wall clock etc. but our ears ignore all of them then a crow comes crowing and sits on the railing of another balcony. This crowing sound diverts my attention to the crow. He picks up a piece of bread and flies away. Here it may be observed that many sounds in the atmosphere could not draw my attention but the crow one because it is louder than others and it has affected my ears. If this sound would have not been louder than others, I might have ignored it too or might have not heard at all. It means there are two types of sounds effects:

1. **General sounds –** These are the sounds in the atmosphere and generally are non-synchronous.

2. **Incidental sounds-** The Sounds are related to an action, procedure or incident and are normally synchronous.

Similar principle is applied in cinema in which 'General sound' provide life to a scene and 'Incidental sounds' emotionally link viewers with various incidents, activities, and procedures taking place in a scene. That's why they are able to feel the effect of such incidents, procedures and activities. If there are no sound effects then one would not hear the sound of footsteps, firing of a bullet, shriek, thunder of the clouds, lightening etc. the visuals without sound will have no effects and the scene will be lifeless. It will have no emotional and psychological impact on the audience. Thus we know the importance of sounds in our life. To feel it close your ears for some time and move around to see what is happening there. You will feel the activities taking place around are life less and ineffective.

It does not mean that whatever sounds are available in the atmosphere or in the ambience, all should be used. If we are standing in a balcony and we are not seeing cars or other vehicular traffic on the road, there is no need for such sounds to be used. In fact if they are used without reference they will disturb the scene. These sounds will not be the center of our attention as there are no visuals corresponding these sounds therefore only those sounds which are effective and attractive and have some bearing in the scene and have corresponding visuals should be used. There are limitations in this principle of the use of sounds for example if two persons are conversing in a moving car, it is not necessary to use the sound of car engine throughout the scene. It could be used in the beginning or in between the gaps and pauses in the dialogues so people will understand that car is moving. Whenever the dialogue starts car sound can be reduced or faded out because audience will be keener and attracted to their conversation. If the car engine sound is not used in the beginning of the scene, there will be something missing and incomplete. If the sound is suddenly cut when the dialogue starts, the cut will be a sound jerk and a disturbance. During the final recording sound levels and transitions should be regulated by reducing the volumes or fading out during a conversation. In the editing of sound 'direct cut' should always be avoided. They can be quick fade in or fade out or a dissolve of sounds.

Sometimes 'Non synchronous sounds' are more important than 'synchronous sounds' because they provide life and reality to visuals. Synchronous sounds are those which are the outcome of an event, incident or an activity and they draw our attention more clearly than those which are part of the atmosphere but are not important enough either for the scene or for our attention. For example when we walk on the road we may not be mindful of running traffic sounds but suddenly get attracted to the sound of a sudden break or a horn that saves us from an impending accident because they can't be ignored as they have some cause and effect on our mind. So it is necessary that whatever is seen, its sound should be used. The Editor should make a search for such sounds in a scene which are effective and have the potential to create more dramatic impact. Our mind picks up only those sounds which are meaningful and have some purpose that's why where a Director works to recreate the reality in combination of visuals and sound, the Editor in association with a Recordist try to re-record them to give them a new meaning. Everyone's objective is only to bring more drama and effectiveness in the film. Viewers see a wall clock on the screen but they have no attention and interest in its tick tock   as it does not provide them any additional information .It is true even in our normal life but in a cinematic scene this tick tock may represent the thought process or indecisiveness of a character or in another scene this tick tock can reflect a conflict between the character and the situation. In addition to the corresponding sounds Director can also use natural or artificially created special sound effects to dramatize a scene. Sound effects can be faded out when not needed that's why a director's cinematic creation should never be only 'visual' but 'audile' so that he can work on a most effective sound track. Sounds are not used only to bring the element of reality but are also used to manage pace and rhythm of the film which requires preplanning to help selection and recreation of appropriate sounds. Those sounds which are digitally or otherwise created should not be sounding artificial; they should be part of the scene and not a separate entity. A sound track different from the visuals of the scene is meaningless. In a 'Montage' scene which is created with the juxtaposition of many disconnected shots, a sound track can work to bind them together. This sound can be music, or some special sound effects to better a transition.

It is observed that cutting fast of the sounds to match the fast cutting of the visuals is not only a challenging task but is also a creative and intellectual decision. It is not necessary to use the similar sounds according to visuals but one has to be cautious when using different sounds which should contribute in the visual unity and emotional effect of the scene otherwise it will lose its meaning and effectiveness. Editor and Director must jointly decide what sounds have to be used. In action sequences like car chase, fights, war etc. it's better to use actual sounds. Many directors use 'symbolic sounds' to enhance the visual and emotional appeal in a scene which is a mix of few disconnected shots like use of 'Howling' to create horror in the night.

The right use of the right kind of sounds which could increase the impact of a scene reflects the creative merits and imagination of a Director and the Editor so due care must be taken to use symbolic sounds. In most of the cases, the sounds used in a scene are according to the background and needs of the story. Experimental sounds reflect subjective creativity of the Director however most film makers give importance to the realistic narration or dialogues unlike covert or symbolic expressions in silent movies. Direct expression is sole choice of film Directors but it is not compulsory for an artistic or experimental film maker to follow a pattern set by others. They differ from one Director to others in their style and presentation which gives them their unique identity, intellectual levels, and vision in storytelling, shot taking, lighting arrangements, editing styles, and use of sounds etc. The number of such films is negligible due to commercial and economical stakes but still there are innumerous possibilities of experimentation with visuals and sounds in a commercial film too therefore it will not be wrong to say that sky is the limit for creative and imaginative expressions for a passionate film maker and a film technician in any department.

It is always better for a Director to preplan the sound track and for the Recordist to provide a good quality of the sound recording. For this purpose a Recordist must understand the dramatic and emotional requirements of the scene then only he will be able to show his creativity. There are no standard parameters for deciding the quality of a sound however a good quality sound is sweet to the ears.

Overlapping of sounds in a dialogue scene is not only required for better dramatic effect but also smoothen the transition. Overlapping of sounds on two talking characters combines their action and reactions particularly in a place where there is no movement between the characters; cut becomes a little difficult for continuity. Here overlapping is a way out for a smooth cut. Similarly with the use of a 'direct cut' of proper sound, a sound transition can be made between two different scenes of similar actions taking place in different locations. For example: closing the door by a character in one location and opening the door by another in other location. In this scene a direct cut can be made by using the sound of closing the door and opening the door in other location. There will be no visual jerk in action by a direct cut. Such cuts display the creativity of the Editor deviating him from the mechanical process to more experimental editing.

*****

Editing is not a straight jacket procedure with many restrictions which cannot be over ruled. Right from the evolution of cinema, Editing too has evolved its own methods and procedures by trials and errors. Editors develop their own style and system to overcome any problem taken place during the shoots.

CUT-5

Editing: Fiction

Since the beginning of cinema the film makers the world over were extensively engaged in experimenting with cinematic techniques and presentation. Starting with 'reality presentation' by Lumiere brothers many mile stones were pitched in to cinematic journey. Deviating from reality coverage, films were made on 'imaginative contents'. Scenes were preconceived and planed. With the arrival of 'Fiction', films on literary, religious, social and folk contents became very popular as the objective of these films was primarily to entertain people. In this efforts music, songs, dances, action, crime, suspense and comedy contents were preferred to cater to the interest of varied social sections. These elements were imbibed in the story. Such films were branded as 'Formula films' in due course of time. Every element had unique presentation so along with the Director, choreographer, Music director, action or stunt director, sound director or sound designer etc. too became an indispensable member of the film crews. These people were specialized in their respective fields. Simultaneously non- fiction genre too developed at a fast pace with the production of News films, Documentary, Promotional and advertisement films etc. When television reached to our drawing rooms many more dimensions were added to the entertainment which gave way to variety of television programs from news and soaps to live shows, stage shows, reality shows, Docu -dramas etc. They are not only different in technique but also in their presentation however they all have a common objective to entertain. Competing with hundreds of television channels maintaining a good 'Television Rating Points (TRP) is a great challenge to television program producers. The way every scene is different in a film, television programs too are different in their contents thus there is a difference in editing styles for both films and television. An Editor therefore should be well versed with the requirements and techniques of television programs as well.

Dialogue sequences:

Most of the fiction films are dialogue oriented. Dialogues not only carry forward the story but also describe characters, their behavior and psyche. In one hand writer pens the dialogues to dramatize and romanticize the scene to make it effective by selecting suitable words and on the other hand Director along with his actors decide on the delivery of dialogues, their movements and the mannerism of the characters to give a strong performance in front of the camera. Most of the dialogues are dull and static. It is only a powerful performance and dialogue delivery of the actors that makes them interesting while shooting. In a conversation scene, talking face to face with in cinematic limitations is not only a compulsion but a necessity of the scene. If actors can bring something new in their delivery of dialogues and performance it is entirely their creativity otherwise these dialogue sequence would become a mere translation of the script. In such a situation it is a challenge for an Editor to edit dialogue scenes effectively. The lighting arrangements, camera movements, acting etc. are important for a dialogue scene to be effective but cutting of the dialogues at the right time and place cannot be ignored. During the delivery of dialogues, actions and reactions of the characters and suitable gaps and pauses work as effective tools to create a more realistic and dramatically interesting scene.

Normally the location where a dialogue is going to start is established in the beginning of the scene proceeding with the introduction of characters in Long shot or a mid shot. When the characters come face to face to each other a combined shot of them is taken. Thereafter their individual dialogues and reaction shots in between their conversation are taken in close shots. There could be some supporting characters in the scene, their actions and reaction shots are also taken as per the requirement. Some time there are some neutral characters in the scenes like party, festivals or gatherings etc. These characters are important to create an ambience. These extra shots are a great help to an Editor when there is wrong dialogue delivery, improper timing, continuity problems etc. Extra shots are used as 'inserts' therefore Director must take as many extra shots as he can while shooting but these shots should be relevant to the ambience and effects.. Mere translation of the dialogue in to the visual form restricts the scope for the Editor to one of the mechanical cutting. He has no solution to correct the mistakes committed during the shoot.

Dialogue scene: Film- Damini

Location- court Room

Characters- Ajay, Damini , chaddha, Judge and the crowed.

1. **Court room, Exterior, Long shot.**
2. **M.L.S. Damini stands in the witness box..Lawyer Chaddha argues in front of the judge pointing to Damini.**

   Chaddha- 'My lord, Damini is very wise and crooked woman. Though she is born in poverty but has always been dreaming big. That's why she charmed and hooked an innocent man like Shekhar...

3. **C.S. Judge listens.**
4. **Same as in shot 2. Damini in the box, Chaddha argues.**

   Chaddha continues- '...In fact she had her eyes set on the wealth of Gupta family. So when in spite of her many attempts she could not grab the locker's keys. She was frustrated. She decided to take revenge with the family for not having her dreams realized.'

5. **M.C.S. Damini looks at the lawyer with shock for his lies.**

   Chaddha-' ... and the enemies of Gupta... family took advantage of the situation...

6. **M.L.S. Ajay, DaminI's Lawyer listens   Chaddha. People are sitting on the rear benches**

   Chaddha-..' And they bought her with money and hatched a conspiracy. They decided to prove that the rape had taken place in Gupta's house to tarnish the reputation of Gupta family....

7. **Same as in 2. Damini in the box, Chaddha argues.**

   Chaddha- 'My lord, it is such a mean act of her.'

8. **Same as 5. Damini in the box.**

9. **C.U. Ajay.**

10. **Same as 2. Damini in the box, Chaddha argues.**

    Chaddha.- 'Sir. This evil woman should be given the severest punishment so other women too get a lesson...'

11. **M.L.S. The Judge is listening.**

    Chaddha- 'That's all, your honor'.

12. **C.S. Chaddha looks at Ajay sarcastically.**

13. **C.U. Ajay smiles.**

14. **M.L.S. Damini in the witness box. Ajay gets up and comes to Damini.-**

    Ajay-'Your Honor, Mr. Chaddha has confused me....'

15. **C.S. Chaddha smiles at Ajay.**

16. **M.L.S. Damini in the box.**

    Ajay speaks- '....It seems he watches too many Hindi films because his case is like any other Hindi films where many stories are jumbled up.'

17. **Same as 15. Chaddha looks at him with anger.**

    Ajay-.'...In the last date Mr. Chaddha told that Damini was mental and today he is telling that Damini is wise and conniving who can scheme. Who can conspire and plan...

18. **Same as 16. Damini in the box.**

    Ajay-. '...In my view my lord, the Girl who is mental cannot be wise and if she is wise, she cannot be mental.'

19. **Same as 11 Judge .**

    Ajay continues- 'therefore my lord I request that Mr. Chaddha too should be sent to mental hospital as Damini for few days at the govt. expenses...'

20. **Long shot. The court room .**

    Ajay- '...so that when he returns back he should confirm if Damini is mental or wise so I can prepare my defense.'

21. **Same as 11. Judge**

22. **Same as 20. Court room.-**

    Ajay-'That's all your honor.'

23.   **C.S. Ajay smiles at Chaddha sarcastically**

24. **Long shot. People in the court room.**

The court scene from the film 'Damini' is a simple and straight Dialogue scene where Editor had very limited options for cutting. Every shot had to be cut as per its length and duration. Reaction shots of Damini, Ajay, the Judge and the people witnessing the proceedings are used to break the monotony of the scene as well as inserts for transition. Director has shot entire dialogues of Chaddha and Ajay as Master shots and single shot reactions of The judge, Damini and people which were intermittently cut in between therefore where shooting is concerned Director has not taken the variety of shots and completed the scene in not more than five shots, the easiest and most economical way of shooting a dialogue scene. The Editor had a challenge to cut the scene in such a way that it did not lose its impact and not become a scene merely of long dialogues therefore splitting the dialogues of Chaddha and Ajay was the only remedy to keep the scene moving. The portions of dialogues have been very appropriately overlapped on the reaction shots to reduce the length and make the scene faster.

Once I happen to see the rushes of a Bollywood feature film. I was amazed to see a two minute scene in a single room, shot from all the possible angles and distances like 'master shots' in long shots, mid shots and close shots. Even reaction shots of each character were taken with prompting of full dialogues in the scene. There was no shot division done prior to the shoot. The two minute scene was shot for almost 210 minutes spread over 20 rolls of 1000ft. each. The total rushes were more than the length of a feature film by any standard. Surprisingly this was done by none other than one of the top and famous film makers of the time and the film had top star cast. I learnt in the film school that shot division must be done prior to any shoot and a ratio of 1:5 was reasonable but here the ratio of 1:105 was almost hundred times more that means for every minute hundred and five minutes film was shot. I could not think of the ratio and total exposed material for the entire film. Later I came to know that most of the film makers did it and left it to the Editor for the final work. Therefore the burden of editing such 'Garbage' was left on his shoulders. Poor Editor was to cut the scene to two minutes is like picking rags from the heaps of garbage. Such things happen during the shootings when the writer ends his job with writing the dialogues without indication of visuals and the Director visually translates those dialogues on celluloid without his creative contribution. This is a reflection of lack of knowledge, creativity, vision and innovation and professionalism. This is the easiest way to shoot a film but not an ideal one. Such scenes lack effectiveness and energy as they are mere translation of the dialogues on screen. It lacks cinematic elements and presentation. This example indicates the problems faced by the Editor while editing . He literally becomes a diver to pick up the best from the huge 'rest'. That's why there should be a detailed directorial as well as editorial planning at the time of writing the screenplay. If writer is satisfied with his imagination and Director is happy with his visualization, the scene could become effective to certain extent otherwise it will just be a screen translation of half heartedly written and conceived scene. Film is a visual medium so cinematic elements while conceiving a scene should never be ignored.

Ramesh Sippy's 'Sholey' is one of the most successful and talked about film in Indian cinema mainly for its dialogues and construction of dialogue scenes and unique visualization and presentation. Over the shoulder shots of characters talking were almost not there. Over the shoulder shots normally indicate hollowness of director's vision and shortage of budget that's why Director tries to wrap up maximum dialogue scenes as over the shoulder shots of the characters talking face to face. Most of the dialogues in the films are the expressions of the characters' personality, their behavior their positive and negative traits and attributes etc. in the following example how the dialogues effectively establish the character of Gabbar Singh, the main antagonist without losing the grip and pace of the scene. The entire scene is shot only on one location of a hilly terrain.

Dialogue scene- Film- Sholey :

Location- A hilly terrain, Day

Characters-Gabbar Singh and his gang men

The scene is an introduction of the antagonist who is also the main character of the film. The scene comes after the gang men of the dacoits Gabbar Singh who is a terror in the area, are hauled out by two young men Jai and Veeru when the gang members went to a village for their routine loot. Jai and veeru assured the villagers not to worry and be scared of Gabbar singh. They single handedly without arms hound them away and warn them not to visit the village again with their nefarious designs. Gabbar Singh feels insulted and challenged for his authority in the region. He is annoyed by the defeat of his gang men samba and Kaila.

1.   **C.U. Camera pans from left to right and shows three dacoits. The feet of Gabbar Singh enter in the frame and move on a rock. Camera follows his feet on a trolley .Metallic effects of shoe steps.**

Gabbar- 'How many people were there?'...only two.

2.   **C.U. Zoom in to the face of Gabbar**

Gabbar- Two men... you sons of pigs.

3.   **C.U. of. Three dacoits.**
Gabber- They was two and you were three then also you came back empty handed. What did you think that boss will be very happy...will complement you... true? Shame on you.

4.   **M.S. To L.S. Zoom out. Camera follows Gabbar from the back of the three dacoits. Gabber sits on the rock.**

147

Gabbar- O Samba, how much head money government has fixed on me.?

5. **Cross angle, three dacoits**
   Samba- full fifty Thousand Boss

6. **M.C.U. Gabbar mixing tobacco on his palm.**
   Gabbar- full fifty thousand. Heard everyone?

7. **L.S. Samba dacoit.**

8. **M.L.S. Composite shot. Gabbar faces the camera and each of the dacoits from the back.**
   Gabbar-Full fifty thousand and this reward is for the fear that fifty miles away from here in a remote village when a child cries then his mother tells him to sleep otherwise Gabbar would come....

9. **Combined shot. Three dacoits**
   Gabbar-You will be punished for it...reasonably punished.

10. **MLS. Gabbar takes out his pistol.**

11. **M.L.S., scared dacoits look at Gabbar.**

12. **L.S.,Gabbar moves to one of the dacoits.**
    Gabbar- how many bullets are there ... how many in this pistol?

    A Dacoit- six, Boss

    Gabbar- There are six bullets in it. Six bullets and three men. It is not judicious.

    Intercut from the view points of the dacoits. Gabbar takes out his pistol when he reaches near them. Gabbar fires three shots in the air.

    Gabbar- Its ok now. There are three bullets in its three dockets and three are empty. Now I will roll it. Now I don't know where the bullets in its three houses are. Which house has bullets and which does not have, I don't know....

13. **M.C.U. to M.S. Gabbar wheels down the mill of the pistol.**

14. **E.L.S. all the dacoits are scared. Zoom out. Gabbar keeps his revolver on one's head**

    Gabbar-now there are three lives and three deaths in this pistol. Let me see who gets what?

15. **Combined shot,Gabbar press the trigger on a dacoit's head.**

    Sound of empty pistol.

    Gabbar- bastard is saved.

16. **Trolley shot. Gabbar triggers on another head. He moves to third dacoit and keeps the pistol on his head. He presses the trigger.**

    Sound of empty pistol.

    Gabbar- He too is saved. what will happen to you, Kalia?

    Kalia-Boss, I have tasted your salt Boss.

    Gabbar- Now have the bullets. (sound of empty pistol)

    Gabbar- it is a miracle.

17. **L.S. all dacoits are laughing**

18. **L.S. Samba Dacoit.**

19. **M.L.S. all three dacoits laugh.**

20. **C.S. two dacoits are laughing**

21. **Back shot of Kalia laughing.**

22. **C.U. two dacoits laugh cautiously**

23. **M.S. Gabbar singh**

24. **L.S. one of the dacoits laughs**

25. **M.S. Gabbar is laughing.**

26. **C.S. Kalia laughs**

27. C.U. separate shots of three dacoits laughing.
28. L.S. Two dacoits laugh
29. Combined shot. All three and Gabbar laugh together.
30. E.L.S. All are laughing.
31. Combined Shot as in 30.
32. M.S. Gabbar suddenly fires at all three of them.
33. C.S. They fall one by one.
34. E.L.S. The last one falls.
35. Zoom. Gabbar spits on his left and goes out.
    Gabbar- The one who is scared is deemed dead.

This scene of 'Sholey' in considered not only a marble of editing but one of the best scenes ever conceived in Indian cinema. Whether it is the dialogue writing, or dialogue delivery, direction or cinematography, sound effects or back ground music, characterization or acting, the scene is different in all angles. I have told you earlier that most of the dialogues are influenced by theatrical techniques where all the characters deliver their dialogues standing in one position with little movements. Camera too concentrates on their faces in close or over the shoulder shots making dialogue delivery very static. Directors too don't make a sincere effort to go to the depth of the characters and the atmosphere.

In the above scene, three dacoits return defeated by Jai and Veeru. This maddens Gabbar Singh with anger. He accuses them for their weakness and narrates a story about his terror in the region saying 'those fifty miles away when a child cries, his mother tells him to sleep otherwise Gabber would come.' The audience too now thinks that the dacoits will not be spared by Gabbar. This is an introduction scene of Gabbar in the film. The scene shot in hilly terrain amid rocks is a reminder Chambal which has been a safe haven of dacoits for decades. The feet in close shot moving on the rocks with metallic sound effects create the right ambience for the scene. In reply of Gabbar's question,' how many were they?' Samba's reply,' only two.' reduces the gravity of unforeseen consequences and lightens the atmosphere giving a bit of relief to the viewers. After that Gabbar's rebuke to the failed dacoits is not more than a display of his ego, power and authority which is necessary and normal to keep his gang intact in such groupings. Gabbar's reference about the reward on his head presents him like a common man with his wide spread influence and power in the distant region. It is not unusual for the viewers to know about the terror of dacoits. His talk about six bullets and three men does not seem to be more than his terror tactics. When all three bullets are fired empty saving the lives of the accused, the scene seems to be over .By their laughter it is attempted to establish that Gabbar is after all not that inhuman as people thought. By this time everyone is assured that worst is over when suddenly all three bullets are fired at them and within moments they fall prey to his bullets. The tension grips the atmosphere once again. Sudden change in his behavior reflects his unpredictability, insensitivity that he could kill anyone unsuspectingly even his loyalists. The character of Gabber is unique comparing to other dacoit characters conceived so far for Indian screen. He is not one of the horse riding gun tottering dacoits who would only order his men nor does he indulge in routine robbery with his people. He is a normal looking careless man with unshaven beard, tobacco mixing, spiting anywhere, without thundering tones etc. He is humorous and jovial with others but one can see terror on his face.

Editing of the scene was preplanned at the writing stage but one cannot deny a credit to the Editor who has heightened the effects with the proper length and timing of the shots. Laughter of dacoits one after another and Gabbar saying that 'all three are saved' gives relief after tense moments and viewers also participate in their happiness. Sudden fire of bullets on them gives a new twist to the tale informing the viewers about his unpredictable behavior. This flip flop of emotions make the scene more interesting and effective that glues the audience with the characters. The script of 'Sholey' is one of the best from editing point of view and contribution of Editor in executing it is remarkable.

Many Producers and Directors of star cast films prefer to expose their stars and use their close ups as much as possible due to commercial reasons and to attract their huge fan following. Very often such situation becomes very embarrassing to an Editor. In the dialogue delivery of stars he cannot do more except reducing or increasing few gaps or intervals here and there. This also poses some problems as many stars have their unique and a definite style and rhythm of performance. Editor's chopping of the gaps can spoil the entire performance of the actor. For example in Bollywood cinema actors like Dilip Kumar and Manoj Kumar are known for their slow dialogue delivery beside taking many pauses in between which if removed may not only ruin their performance but render the entire scene ineffective. This may annoy the ardent supporters of the stars who are deprived of watching their special performance. In this situation the Editor should cut the scene very carefully without affecting the general pace of the film and the performance of actors without disturbing their timing. While Editor may cut the negative elements of an actor's performance, he can also improve their performance by sleek editing.

It is generally observed that a Director concentrates more on other scenes like an action scène, song and dance numbers etc. than a dialogue scene because he thinks that he has nothing much to do in a dialogue scene and it will be carried out easily by an actor and the cameraman.. That's why we don't see much of a Director's imagination and the scenes become flat. This step motherly treatment to a dialogue scene is not conducive to the overall quality of the scene. In dialogue scenes the main attraction is 'Catchy words' and the ' Punch lines' which linger in the memory of the audience for longer time and close ups or combined shots of stars are enough to enthrall the viewers.

After films the Television has emerged as one of the most potent medium of entertainment. Most of the television serials are influenced by cinema Techniques except that Television is called a 'close up medium' due to its small screen and less viewing distance. Therefore long shots are normally not very effective and only medium and close shots are workable. This makes a Television serial more a dialogue oriented. Lack of visual variety is clearly visible and it restricts an Editor to display his creativity. Other limitations come in the form of TRP, lack of knowledge and professionalism in television technicians including an Editor. It is commonly evident to have visual disconnect, jerk in looks, movements and in the use of actions and reactions. 'Filmic time' is the greatest casualty which is reduced and extended without reasonable limits. It is one of the main reasons why many Television serials are not able to have a long term viewership and are prematurely withdrawn from telecast. It is said earlier that films or television are not reality but a feeling of realism. Therefore the television content should also move as is real with minor alteration in pace and timing. If there is a break in psychological formation of characters and the situation beyond a threshold limit, it becomes ineffective. It is the Editor's responsibility to work out proper continuity, timing and relation between actions and reactions and for no excuses he can be absolved of his profound duty.

Comedy sequences:

Humor is very important in our lives. There would be no one who does not like to laugh. Entertainment through comedy is a habit that develops on its own since childhood. Our children enjoy watching cartons or comedy programs on Television. We may remember our own childhood when we liked to read or hear wits and comics. There were dedicated columns for humor in news papers and periodicals. The Humor was and is still very popular among poets who recite their satirical and comic poetry. Even as adults many take it to their profession to make others laugh. In circus Jokers were very important for the success of their show. Many used to visit a circus only to enjoy the fun presented by Jokers. In cinema actors in comedy roles used to act and deliver their dialogues in ridiculous manners. There was at least one comic actor in every film to bring relief through humor. There mere presence in the film was enough to bring peal of laughter on the faces of viewers. These comedy actors were no less than a star in their field.

Chaplin, Laurel and Hardy, Johnny walker, Mehmood, Kishore Kumar and many more who gave a new definition and an identity to comedy. They later became cult figures and comedy became another genre of entertainment. While in earlier cinema comedy was used as a filler to 'change of mood' with few scenes in a film. These scenes had no connection with the main storyline and their main objective was to make people laugh by their amusing and foolish tricks. Later on films with full comic contents became popular and comic actors carved out their own individual identify. A new viewership came in to existence to support comedy films. In India, films like 'Chalti Ka Naam Gadi', Johar Mehmood in Goa', 'Kunwara Baap', 'Padosan' etc became the classical comedies in Indian cinema. Later directors like Hrishikesh Mukherjee opted to produce light hearted films with dignified comedy. His films 'chupke Chupke', Bawarchi', are still remembered by cine goers. His characters were not comedians but they created situational humor. Raj Kapoor, the great Indian showman, was known for his slapstick comedy. He gave a new twist to comedy characters that not only busted laughter but also created sympathy for them. His film 'Mera Naam Joker' is a mile stone in Indian cinema. In later years many more film makers added their names in the list.

There is a general feeling that 'making people laugh' is very easy but it is not so. Creating laughter for one or many is one of the toughest tasks. Sometimes a wit or a joke may cheer someone but at the same time it may have less or no effect on others. It depends on the 'attitude' or an I.Q, of the viewers. For some comedy contents seem to be childish, foolish or cheap and for some it can be source of being happy. So there is no standard formula or a principle possible for comedy .Now the foremost question comes in our mind as to what are the situations which create humor or we can have peal of laughter. Any comedy how so ever good it is can be marred by a bad execution.

There is a remarkable difference in cutting styles for a serious and a comedy sequence. In serious contents cutting is done following the technical principles required for neat, peaceful and realistic approach. A deviation in technical rules becomes evident in lack of continuity and resulting distraction from the main content affecting its overall presentation. Technical compromises in serious contents are made only when they are necessary and required for special effects. While in comic situations anything and everything is acceptable which creates humor and laughter. Serious contents have long lasting effects on the mind while comedy is very short lived. Therefore harsh cuts, continuity jerks or any other unusual situations are acceptable and Editor can take technical liberties if his cuts create comedy. With sounds in films comedy actor depend more on delivering jokes on screen. The success of their jokes depends on their presentation, style and sense of timing. Editor can only provide them a 'tempo' or 'sleek speed' to be more effective. The actors in comic roles enjoy complete freedom to work on their wits and actions and decide on their timing, behavior, mannerism and presentation. The role of a Director or an Editor is negligible and it is not proper for them to interfere in their acts.

While editing a comedy scene Editor must give a little pause for laughter in between the jokes to avoid overlapping of a long one on other. It is better to balance them so that laughter is continued on the jokes one after another. It is possible that some jokes may not create ripple or the pause is so long to lose its effect. Sometimes a weak joke in the middle of few others too may create a desired laughter. Against the witty dialogue scenes, in the situational comedy scenes the role of a Director and an Editor becomes important. Most of the comedy scenes are limited to certain actions like throwing cream on the faces, hurting and pushing, comic stunts etc. in such scenes 'timing' and sleek editing is very important. Careless cutting may ruin the comedy. Therefore Director and Editor should be aware at the time of the shoots as to what will create more laughter.

Think of an example of David Lean-

1. **Medium Long Shot- Laurel and Hardy are running on a road, after about 15 second's run Hardy slips and falls down,**
2. **Close up- A banana peel is on the road. After some time Hardy's foot falls on it and he slips down,**

It seems that it would be better to cut the shot of banana peel after the entry of Hardy's feet in the frame. Showing the slip half way if it is cut to Medium long shot falling of Hardy would be proper. Both the cuts will be fine. When Hardy falls people will laugh but the laughter may not be longer. The answer lies in the following principle of creating maximum laughter-

1   Prior intimation of the action.
2   Do what you want to do,
3   Then inform that it is done.

With the above principle the scene could be edited somewhat like this-

1. Medium Shot- Laurel and Hardy are running on the road.
2. Close shot-Banana peel is lying on the road. (By showing the banana peel, you inform the viewers what is going to happen. Viewers start laughing in anticipation of a fall.)
3. Medium Shot- Laurel and Hardy are still running on the road. (They don't know what is going to happen. It increases the laugher. They should be shown running before they fall.)
4. Close shot- Hardy's feet enters in the frame and slips on the peal.
5. Medium Shot- Hardy looks at Laurel with embarrassment. (Viewers laugh louder.)
6. Close shot- Laurel looks at Hardy innocently.

Normally it is observed that people enjoy other peoples' agony, particularly of obese men, as happened with Hardy. Instead of having sympathy for him they enjoy his fall. According to the principles of comedy Editor creates the same situations for Hardy where people can laugh. In shot 2 viewers are informed about what is going to happen with Hardy and they get prepared to enjoy the impending action and Hardy's helplessness. This also gives them a feeling of superiority that they know something which Hardy does not know. This makes Hardy inferior because viewers know about banana peel while Hardy is ignorant. This feeling of superiority increases the sense of their entertainment. The few moments prior to his fall in shot 3 increase the expectant joy. Hardy's embarrassment in shot 5 and Laurel's innocent look at him take the laughter to its climax. This editing pattern of a very common situation could be considered the best in presentation and effectiveness of a comic situation among any other options editor could explore provided it has the same or more laughter.

With the change of times, the forms of comedy changed too. Earlier comic actors entertained people by their antics, ridiculous costumes and foolish dialogues and jokes. The comedians were used as comic relief to break the monotony of the film. The comic actors were billed as 'supporting actors' much below the star status of the main leads. These comedians usually played the roles of a friend, brother or sister of the main characters and were with them in happy and critical times that are why their presence in the film was not forced however their contribution in the main content was insignificant. It was a challenge for comic actors to entertain people in limited time and scenes. Gradually there was a growing demand for comedy films with a dedicated viewership for such films. Some big names in the film profession joined the bandwagon of comedy films that raised the standard of comedy beyond the wits and antics to situational comedy. Actors of these films were basically not comic actors but they seriously worked to entertain people. The comedy imbibed in the content and the dialogues of these films. Stars like Amitabh Bachchan, Dharmendra, Raj Kapoor, Rishi Kapoor, Shammi Kapoor, Biswajeet and many more were ever eager to play comic roles. With such stars in comedy roles the aura of comedy widened from side lines to the main stream cinema. Their audience too did not remain confined to a limited number but enlarged to cross higher limits consisting of all ages and social sects. Technically there was no special cutting pattern for comedy films but was edited like any other films except that special attention was given to the timing of actions and reactions and avoids unnecessary gaps and pauses. Actors were too expected to maintain proper timing in their deliveries. Pre planning at the time of writing script is very important for a comedy film so making a comedy film should never be taken lightly by anyone from the writer to the director and actors to the editor.

The following example of the film 'Race' presents a comic actor like a character in the film that is not less than the main character in the scene. Anil Kapoor, Johny Liver and Lara Datta reach to the office of the Registrar of Marriage.

Comedy scene: Film- Race

Location: Marriage Registrars office

Characters: Anil, Johnny and Lara

1. **C.U. Display board of 'Registrar of Marriage'**
2. **Trolley shot. Anil and Lara enter in the office of the registrar and move to the reception. Anil looks to his left.**
   Anil-'Mr. Max'
   Receptionist- Please have seat. He will be here in five minutes'.
   Anil- Thank you
3. **L.S. Empty Space. We overhear Johnny**
   Johnny- I am not a slave of your father. You have not obliged me if you have delivered children.I told you not to disturb me in my office. Ihave some reputation here, understand?
4. **M.L.S. Anil and Lara come towards the camera.**
5. **L.S. both of them come and stands near a table**

6. **M.L.S. Johnny enters from the back of the wall talking on his mobile.**

   Johnny-will you complain to my father? You are my wife and remain like that. Shut up.

7. **Trolley shot. Anil and Lara sit on the chairs. Johnny stops near his table talking on his phone.**

8. **M.S. Johnny towards the camera. Back Shot-Anil and Lara are on their chairs.**

9. **M.C.S. Anil and Lara sit in front.**

   Anil- sir, we....

   Johnny- (cuts in between) Have to marry...?

10. **M.S. Johnny (as in shot 8)**

11. **M.L.S. O/S Anil and Lara looks at Johnny towards camera**

    Johnny-see these days boys and boys, girls and girls are getting married. What happened to you and which bug has bitten you?

12. **C.U Johnny**

    Johnny- I say instead of bringing a wife by marriage.... See don't mind...

13. **As in shot 9 Anil and Lara look at Johnny**

    Johnny- instead of bringing a wife by marriage.

14. **C.U. Johnny as in shot 12.**

    Johnny- Buy a mobile and talk.

15. **As in shot 9.Anil and Lara**

    Johnny- Mobile will not be angry. Don't mind sister...

16. **Johnny's in shot 12**

    Johnny- You can keep it in silence but how will you silence your wife?

17. **Anil and Lara looks at him as in shot 11**

    Johnny-You can change its ring tone. I say, don't mind sister.

18. **Johnny as in shot 12**

    Johnny-Wife cannot be controlled, mobile can be in your grip.

19. **Anil and Lara as in shot 9**

    Johnny- you can keep it in your pocket… you can exchange it too, give the old and take the new one.

20. **Johny As in shot 11**

    Johnny- wife is a chewing gum… wife is a chewing gum.

21. **Johny as in shot 9 Anil forwards a bottle of chewing gum to him**

    Johnny- wife is a chewing gum… wife is a chewing gum.

22. **Johnny as in shot 12. He picks one and start chewing.**

    Johnny-Thank you. It is sweet in the beginning than continue masticating.

23. **M.C.S. as in shot 9. Anil and Lara chew gum. Johnny gives them a form.**

    Johnny- if you also want to chew for life time then fill up this form.

24. **M.C.S. As in shot 9. Anil and Lara.**

    Anil- sir, myself R.D…..

25. **Johnny- as in shot 12**

    Johnny- (cuts him) RD Burman, music director…

26. **Johnny as in shot 9.**

    Johnny- oh, I am a big fan of you. I love listening your music.

    Anil- I am not that RD.

27. **C.U. Johnny is disturbed.**

    Johnny- Annnn...

28. Anil and Lara As in shot 9

Anil- RD means Robert de Costa. Inspector Robert de Costa.

29. C.U. Johnny is now afraid of him. He defends himself.

Johnny- My wife has sent you sir? We only have quarrels. I am not a criminal. I am a good man sometimes there is a misunderstanding.

30. Anil and Lara As in shot 9.Anil and Lara are sitting in front of him.

Anil- I have come here for a case.

Comparison of a wife with a mobile by Johnny and repeatedly asking her 'don't mind sister' makes the scene entertaining and laughable. Then his comparison with a chewing gum makes the scene very casual and humorous. Anil's introduction to him as an Inspector frightens Johnny; this makes the scene highly humorous enabling people to burst into laughter. The location of the office of the Registrar of marriages and Johnny amalgamate with each other like water in the milk and the scene becomes part of the main content as it does not look like an isolated one. It may be observed that the entire scene is shot and restricted to only two shots 9 and 12. Editor did not play with the timing of Johnny but he created comedy only by intercutting these two shots of the comedy character thus becomes part of the main scene.

Earlier there were few film makers who were dedicated to making comedy films. Though they were few in numbers but they had their own identity and respect as director. They were commercially successful so it was not difficult for them to rope in the stars. These film makers had developed a wide audience for comedy films. Due to limited budget these films were able to recover their cost. It inspired many other film makers to enter in to production of comedy films. The commercial success of comedy films in fact became an entry point for many first time producers as they saw sure success in this genre. Now any small or a big star is ready to play a comic character. Comic actors are no more a second fiddle to lead characters. From Shahrukh Khan to Ajay Devgan, from Salman to Amir, from Govinda to sunil shetty and from Amitabh Bachchan to Anil Kapoor they all have greased their faces for a comedy film and enjoyed it. There were many comedy films made recently such as welcome, Partner, Socha Na tha, Jab we met, Oh my God,, PK, Atithi tum kab jaoge, Malamal and Golmal series of films etc. were not only appreciated but had established comedy as a genre in Indian cinema. Now day's comedy films are much sought after films than any other content. As a matter of fact the present generation is the main sponsor of these films.

These films are written and conceived as comedy and Artistes are selected according to the requirement of the characters. Most of these artistes are not branded or known comedians. The editing of these films is also planned while writing the screen play giving more conceptual clarity to an Editor.

Comedy in Television:

Extending its reach from films comedy has also made television its forte in a big way. The comedy in television has its distinct identity with its dedicated viewership. In the lighter moments at home watching light hearted programs has suitable back drop. These programs serve dignified comedy and healthy entertainment to the television viewers of all ages, gender and sections. Television has provided comedy an opportunity to diversify from foolish dialogues and ridiculous antics to make a comments on our society, culture, politics, national and international issues etc. in the form of satires and taunts to awaken the sleeping consciousness of our viewers. In fact these programs reflect the interest, anger, change and expectations of our people which are considered to be the main reason for their success.

Television has two types of programming- one fiction based series and other recording of live events which could be 'real' or 'staged' shows. Though many series are shot with a single camera unit, there are multiple camera set up required for 'Live recordings'. Many producers use multi-camera set up for shooting of a serial to save in time and money however those film makers who are migrated to television still prefer single camera set up as this gives them more creative freedom. In multi-camera set up normally used for live coverage, Director does not have much scope for maneuvering during the live action which cannot be interrupted for any reason. The cameras deployed at various vintage points continue to record the event as it proceeds however the Director controls the camera through a vision mixing unit and simultaneously edit the program during the course.

Vision Mixer is a digital device in which the Editor cuts a shot as directed by the Director. The problem in the digital editing is that there is always a gap between the director's instructions and the editor's cutting that shifts the cutting point slightly and the cut is not as smooth as it should be. Since there are multiple cameras working at a time cutting from one camera to another have many other flaws like difference in the direction of looks, artistes' movement, angles, and tonal jerks etc. However since viewers attention is centered on the program, such distraction is not disturbing. Director too has to be ready with another cut while one shot is still running on the screen. All the cameras continue shooting without interruption and move as per the back room instructions from him. There is no black out while camera is on as something will always be seen on the screen therefore a jerk in cutting is not noticed. The editing of live program is not editing oriented but presentation oriented one that includes writing and performance of participants. Any maneuvering sometimes is possible if it is a 'deferred telecast' which means that recording and telecast dates are different however nothing much can be done in the program if telecast simultaneously. If the program is shot with a single camera set up, the same principles and methods are applied in their editing as are followed for a film.

 Technical restrictions in Television production, shooting with multi-camera set up and lack of technical knowledge among creative team members including directors are some of the drawbacks that we see some blunders in continuity in television programs. These flaws are mainly evident in the direction of looks of anchors and participants in the talk shows, change in the entry and exit directions in the frame, crossing of imaginary line in over the shoulder shots etc. The television producers must come out of the sense that viewers don't know anything, yes, they may be right but viewers are not supposed to know the technicalities therefore for the sake of quality they should stop them taking for granted as subconsciously they are able to make out the flaws though technically they are not able to define or specify them. This subconscious impact reflects in TRP by their rejection of the program. Directors must also realize that viewers hold remote control to decide among hundreds of television channels and thousands of programs what program they would see and what they would not if the program is not up to their expectations.

Action sequences:

Action sequences were prevalent since the time of silent cinema but then meaning of an action was mostly a 'chase.' in which one or more people used to chase another person or a group. In most of the films the Hero or the police chased the villain or criminals. These scenes were edited in fast pace to create interest, entertainment and romance. The Editor should be careful while editing an action sequence that 'chaser' and 'chased' should not confuse viewers by arbitrary changing the direction of their movements or angles which defy imaginary line. To avoid this confusion the shots must be selected and cutting be done in such a way that chaser and chased maintain proper distance. The distance between them can be reduced citing some reasons so the chase does not run ahead of the chased. If it happens it reverses the role of chaser and chased for no reason. Therefore some Long shots in between to reiterate their respective positions should be cut very often. If there is a change of place or the direction of the movement from left to right or right to left, a shot establishing the change with proper justification must be used otherwise sudden change will create confusion.

The cinematic convenience to take audience to various places where simultaneous action take place is one of the many important factors to create interest and romance in a film sequence. Due to this cinematic liberty many films in various genres like Mystery, war, crime and action films are produced regularly. These films are normally fast paced action drama in which speeding vehicles and characters, chase, fight, and stunts dominate the main content. There is a dedicated category of audience for such films. In Indian cinema Nadia, Dara singh, Shetty, Sanjeeev Kumar, Kamran and many others were very popular action stars of yester years. In due course other stars from mainstream cinema too started working in action films and they were called 'Action Hero'. Similar to comedy, action films too were recognized as mainstream commercial films. The action films which always fought for a respectable budget earlier were being considered at par with other high budget films starring big actors. They were no longer restricted to C class but competed with other big ticket ventures. This development also saw the technical up gradation of action films. The digitally generated special effects revolutionized the action in 3 Dimension and 4 Dimension. In fact the digital visual effects are mostly created for Action scenes therefore these films made with astronomical budget are technically of outstanding quality that can be compared with any international production.

Action scene: Film 'Sholey.

'Sholey' has been rated as one the best action film in the history of Indian cinema where action was done by stars like Amitabh Bachchan, Dharmendra and sanjeev Kumar among others. These action sequences were conceived and directed by specially invited foreign action directors. That's why

'Sholey's actions are still appreciated and remembered for their technical excellence and stunts. In this action scene the Police officer Sanjeev Kumar takes two handcuffed petty criminals in a goods train when they are attacked suddenly by dacoits.

1. The train stops in the desert.
2. M.S. Police officer looks out.
3. M.S. composite shot. Profile. Jai and Veeru peep out of the train window.
4. M.S. Police officer looks out
5. M.S. camera in the tunnel. The engine driver is thrown out of the tunnel.
6. M.S. wide angle. Intercut.. The driver is falling out of the engine. another driver
   Turns back to see him when he is also hit by a bullet. And he too falls out on another side.
7. C.S .Police officer looks out holding his pistol when he feels a jerk and is about to fall. The train moves.
   Officer-- Dacoits....?
8. E.C.S. Train wheels move fast.
9. M.C.S. o/s a dacoit keeps his gun on the driver.
10. C.S. a constable looks out and falls instantly with a shriek. Pan Jai and Veeru watch him falling.
11. C.S. Officer fires from the running train Jai and Veeru are seen further.
    Firing. Shriek,
    Jai- where is your bravery now, officer?
12. C.S. Officer fires from the running train Jai and Veeru are seen further.
13. C.S. Pan, officer comes in. Jai and Veeru show him their handcuff. Both are tied with one handcuff.

Veeru- officer, there is still some time. Think it over.

14. C.U. of the officer. He looks at their hands which are handcuffed. Officer fires a bullet on it. Both are freed. Officer runs out.

Back ground music, Firing,

Officer- but don't ever try to escape.

15. M.S. Tilt up. Veeru and Jai stand up and run out of frame from different sides.

16. C.U. Veeru's feet tilt up with Veeru climbing on a stair.

17. C.S. Veeru climbs on the top of a compartment

18. E.C.S. Tilt up from the feet of Veeru. He is running on the bogeys.

19. L.S. Veeru runs forward after climb up

20. M C.U. Veeru stands up on a blank frame and looks left.

21. M..S. Veeru runs towards the camera on a running train.

22. C.U. Veeru stands up on a blank frame and looks left.

23. M.L.S. camera on the running train.at the outer a dacoit is chasing on a horse.

24. M.L.S. low angle pan shot. Another dacoit is on the horse chasing on other side.

25. C.S. Veeru looks at a dacoit and runs after him.

26. M.S. a dacoit points his gun to the camera

27. M.S. oil vessels are kept on both sides of the camera.

28. E.L.S. two of the dacoits are running on their horses on both sides of the train. Pan left another three come on their horses towards the train.

29. CU.Veeru climbs up on a bogey. camera pans right. Dacoit moves to Jai. Veeru hits him by his feet on his chest.

Veeru- Driver, stop the train.

30. M.S. Veeru jumps out of the bogey.

31. C.S. scared driver looks around and down the handle.

32. M.L.S.Veeru fights with a dacoit and another tries to stop the train.

M.L.S. Driver looks out. Veeru comes to him to say to move fast.

Veeru- Run the train as fast as possible. When a dacoit comes from his back and tries to separate him with the driver. They fight.

33. L.S. pan camera is in the train. Few dacoits on their horses are chasing with the train. Pan right many more dacoits come towards the running train

34. M.S. Composite shot. Officer and Jai look at the dacoits.

35. L.S. dacoits run on their horses few more join them.

36. C.S. a dacoit pushes Veeru by his face to the engine fire.

37. M.S. Veeru forcefully pushes him away by his feet.
Veeru- you....run away.

38. M.S. exterior, the dacoit falls down after the beating.

39. Composite M.S. zoom officer and Jai look at him. Officer comes in and Jai points his gun,

40. C.U. running wheels.

41. E.L.S. The train passes through a river

42. M.I.S.a group of dacoits chase on their horses

43. L.S. Low angle. Dacoits come to the camera. They leave from left and right of the camera.

44. L.S. wide angle. After the driver is hit by a bullet, Veeru asks him to sit aside. A M.L.S. trucking shot. Interior, Dacoits chase the train outside.

45. Onwards up to shot166 Repeat actions.

.   46. C.U. Veeru looks at chasing dacoits

47.M.S. dacoits run away on their horses.

48.. C.S. zoom out Jai looks at running   dacoits. Veeru
keeps his hand on Jai saying.

> Veeru- Bastards ran away.
> Jai- yes of course.

The most interesting fact of this action is that the entire scene
is shot on a running goods train and horses. There is
movement in every shot so there is no static moment. This is
also an introduction scene of the film that introduces the main
characters Police officer, Jai and Veeru and their personalities,
their attributes and their habits. Veeru is a brave man who
does not care for his life, Jai is calm but brave. The police
officer is good at recognizing people that's why he breaks
open their handcuff with a trust and instruction that they
should not run away. The meticulous picturisation of the scene
has made Editor's job easy as the scene has its own speed but
still the length of the shot matters to maintain a uniform pace.
Selection of shots and proper placement is Editor's creative
contribution to develop an effective scene.

In most of the action in chase sequences the viewers are
aware about the end result. It reduces their interest and
romance in the scene. This situation is very challenging not
only for the Director but also for the Editor. It is always very
difficult to create interest in disinclined viewers. To overcome
this problem Directors try to bring variety in action, chase and
stunt scenes and Editor too tries to bring variety in cutting
style by using actions and reaction of other characters, some
accident or by using technical tools for special visual effects to

generate interest. Editor tries to ensure that the scene does not slow down. For this purpose high decibel sound effects and back ground music is used to keep the audience awake and desist from yawning. Parallel actions and opposite actions are another way out of this problem. Every shot seems different and new than earlier ones. Though there is no rule for using variety of shots, in action sequences close shots are more effective than long shots so use of close shots must be adhered to a much as possible without diverting and confusing from the main plot. For continued interest in the scene Editor should keep on fluctuating the pace of the scene as the same pace for a long time may be monotonous. Reactions from static characters can be used to fill the gaps to vent viewer's reactions through other characters. It is very often observed that viewers start expressing their feeling in the same manners as the characters in the scene behave, on seeing a particular action and reaction. Editor can use various shots of the same action taken from different angles and distances to maintain the interest.

The final effect of an action scene largely depends upon the Editor however it is very difficult to guess about it at the planning stage but Director should anyway preplan the type of actions and stunts required in the scene and take some extra shots along with the main action. These extra shots are required by the Editor to fill the gaps and avoid continuity jerks therefore an Editor should be provided as much material as possible which he can use to create the desired effect. Similar situation arises in war sequences or an accident or on human calamities where multiple cameras are used to cover the scene where no cameraman is aware about the use of his coverage. Whatever is seen by him is captured in his camera.

So Editor has so much material at his command that he can use it the way he wants. Irrespective of the manners shooting is done, the responsibility of achieving power packed pace and speed and continuity lies on the Editor.

Editor has more creative freedom to edit action sequences than the dialogue scenes. In dialogue scene Editor is guided by the pace and length of the dialogues, actors' movements, script and predefined editing pattern which he has to follow indiscreetly. Howsoever well planned an action scene is there would be no shot connected with each other. Every shot has its own meaning and the purpose which editor can interpret the way he wants and display his creative merits.

Music and musical sequences:

Music plays a very important role in cinema in general and in fiction films in particular. It is an important ingredient of fiction films either in the form of song and dance performances or as back ground score. Songs and dances are part of Indian culture however it does not mean that cinema of other countries and society is devoid of them. They too use them as situational requirement which become part of the ambience but in Indian cinema music has always been used to entertain in whatever form it may be. There is music for every occasion in Indian society whether it is sad or happy, there is music for all seasons like rains or spring, there is music for all emotions like for love and affection, for isolation and gatherings, there is music for farming and festivals, there is music from the birth of a child to the death of a person etc. that's the reason since the beginning of cinema in India Music was always an important component of cinema. Music in Indian society has been a form of expression for all ages and gender. With the sound coming in to films, film makers were overwhelmed with the opportunities it provided to use music in cinema. It was one of the reasons that actor –singers were the preferred choice to play the lead roles so that they can sing, dance and acts at the same time. KL Sehgal, Noorjehan, Suraiya, Pankaj Malik and many more, were very popular singing stars of their time. Mukesh and Mohammad Rafi too acted in some of the films. Continuing this tradition of singing actors Kishor Kumar, Sulakshana Pandit and many more joined the band wagon of the Play back singing and revolutionized Indian music which had altered the presentation and technology of music sequences. Like other scenes shot division for songs and dance sequences became a norm unlike earlier times when the entire song and dance was shot in one go in a single shot. Shot division for musical sequences is done in the similar manners as for others by incorporating different angles, different distances and different movements of artists. Songs and dances are used by film makers to refresh the mood of the audience to break the monotony or give them a relief. There is also a commercial angle attached to musical sequences. Popularity of songs in the film not only helped in the success of the film but it has also brought significant returns on their investments. In due course Music had become a source of extra revenue for the producers by way of music sales, performance rights, broadcast rights etc. so now having good music in the film has become more a financial compulsion than the requirement of the film content with steep rise in the budget for Music.

Songs and dances:

The songs and dances in fiction films are expressions of personal feelings and emotions of love, union and separation, happiness and sorrow. These emotions are given words by a lyricist or a poet which are composed by Music director. These compositions are generally a feast to the ears and touch our hearts. The popularity of these compositions is gauged by the feet that start tapping when the music is played; composition is hummed when it hits the ears. There is always a demand for performing the same on stage appearances of the performers whether they are actors, singers or the music directors. The sky rocketing sales chart is another parameter for the success of music. Sometimes the same music becomes classics and attains the tag of being 'Evergreen'. Some of them become 'Immortal' in the music history. Such compositions reflect the passion of writers and music composers. They become a challenge and a piece of extreme satisfaction for the Editor and Director. The picturisation of musical performances is completely opposite and different than other scenes in which Director's role is insignificant as they are shot by a choreographer who has expertise in nuances of music and dance performances. The choreographers are efficient in translating the musical rhythms and moods in to the physical expressions and movements of the performers. The entire musical track is divided by the choreographer in to number of shots as per the musical beats and required actions of the performers.

There is no fixed procedure for preparation of musical sequences. Sometimes a lyricist writes the words on a situation and the music director composes the music before it is shot on the actors. Sometimes composition is prepared first and words are fit into the music later, this procedure by no means is an ideal one but indeed it is more popular as it gives freedom to composers to compose the way they want. This procedure has become easier with the use cords in the music composition where much of the work of the composer is automatically done by the press of the button. After the composition the singer renders his voice while recording the same in the studio. In the earlier years the music recording was done at stretch and repeated again if there was a slightest mistake either in instrumentation or in singing but now the recording has become more a piece meal activity for the recording crew. While it achieves a greater technical perfection, it has lost the soul, seriousness and passion of the composing and recording teams.

Similarly it is a different ball game to edit the musical performances. The way dialogues scenes are edited according to the movements of the actors and the duration of the dialogues, a musical performance is edited according to 'beats' and 'rhythm'. To do this an Editor must have developed some sense and knowledge of music. After recording, the choreographer visualizes various actions and movements based on the composition, its rhythm and pace and the meaning and mood of the lyrics. Where ever there is only an orchestra, he decided the shots as per the change-overs. Actions are changed as per the locations. During the shoot every song or dance performance is played back for the performers to act as per the composition. The assistant choreographer rehearses the movements of every step before the commencement of shooting. When they all are ready they go for a 'take'. During the shoots, extra shots and insertions of the main and other performers are taken to facilitate the Editor's requirement for continuity in editing. It may be understood that the rhythm of the musical performance depends on the composition. If the composition is slow the pace will be slow, if it is faster, it will be fast. An artificially created slow pace for fast composition and fast pace for a slow composition is disastrous and unacceptable and an Editor should keep it in mind and choose shots for cutting accordingly.

It is always observed that whenever we hear our favorite number we start tapping and our body parts start dancing on their own. Our beats are in total synchronization. An interruption in it irritates us. Similarly the Editor should also understand that every cut is made as per the beats so as to synchronize it with the audience beats. If there is interference or the cut is not in synch with beats it will disturb the viewers. Therefore before the editing of a musical sequence the Editor should 'mark' every beat on the sound track so after assembling the rushes he would make the cut on the nearest beat. If there is a continuity issue he must make use of inserts and extra shots but in no case he should make a cut off the beat. It does not mean that every beat should have a cut but whenever there is cut it should possibly be on a beat. Similarly it is also not necessary that every change over should have a cut however choreographers always try to change a shot on a changeover. There could be many actions in a shot or there can be a camera movement on a changeover or where there should be a cut, it's the creativity of the choreographer how he divides his shots in a musical performance and devises the movements compatible to the rhythm and pace of the number.

Sometimes a brief change over or a variation in the music peace may not be on the beats but it does not disturb because it is taken care of by the change over in Music which matches with the change in the action. Sometimes an Editor has to use a cut for some technical reasons which may not fall on a beat or a change over; it this case shot is kept very short and 'subsequent cut' again falls on a beat. Though such cuts are necessary sometimes, Editor must avoid as much as possible to avoid interruption in the mental rhythm of the music which audience continuously tap on their feet.

Back ground Music:

The musical performances on the screen directly entertain people while the back ground music is used only to create some emotional effects that are compatible with the scene. The back ground music can be created for specific purpose or can be adopted from the 'folks'. It is the Music director who takes a decision about the requirements and the type of music for the scene however it is the Editor who decides how to use the same. Back ground music should never be used as a 'filler'. it is not appropriate and is deplorable. The music has its own effect which in combination with visuals enhances the effect of the scene. If inappropriately used, music loses its melody and it becomes noisy. The way a Director works on the script ,Music director works on the music once the rough cut of the film is ready. Back ground music should be used only to increase the impact of the scene otherwise let the scene remain without music. In the absence of back ground music sound effects may be more effective and appropriate. Sometimes even 'silence' is better to have a desired effect.

Back ground Music: Film-Toote Pankh

This is the introduction scene of the film 'Toote Pankh' by Kuldeep Sinha. In this scene Dayal returns to his ancestral home when he is retired from his service after many years. He had a full and happy family which got disintegrated in due course. It saddens him and he decides to come back to his place after the demise of his wife. Today he returns as a lonely man. He is depressed at the turn of events in his life.

1. **L.S.on a narrow pathway of a village a horse cart is running**- Sound of horse hoofs continues till the cart stops.
2. **M.L.S.an old man Dayal is in deep thought inside the cart.**
3. **M.L.S. opposite angle. The cart puller goads the horse to run faster**.
4. **L.S. View point shot. Camera follows the road from the running cart.**
5. **Top Angle shot. View point. Of the road.**
6. **C.S. Dayal is in thoughts. Cart is running**
7. **L.S. the cart coming from the distance stops in front of an old bungalow. Cart sound stops**.
8. **M.L.S. Dayal gets down and stands looking the bungalow. A servant picks up his luggage and opens the lock.** Sound of birds and dogs.Lock opening sound.
9. **C.S. Dayal looks at his bungalow quietly.**
10. **L.S. slow pan shot of the bungalow.** Soft Back ground music fades in and fades out when the shot is completed .
11. **C.S. as in no, 9. Dayal looking at the house.**

12. **L.S., the servant invites Dayal to enter the house. He reaches near the door.**

13. **M.S. Dayal opens the door. Door opening sound.**

14. Top angle. L.S. Interior, The door opens from inside the hall. The pigeons flutter around. Spider's nets are seen around. Dayal switches on the lights. cracking sound of the old door. Pigeons Flutter.Sound of the electric switche and fluttering..

15. **C.S. Light is on in the hall. Broken wings of the pigeons are falling in the frame.**

16. Film's Title

17. **M.S. Dayal moves in and looks at a dusted family photo kept in the corner. He looks at it. Pigeons flutter.**

18. **M.L.S. Dayal picks up the photo and cleans the dust. Camera zooms to the photo.**

19. Flash Back. Camera zooms from a bunch of balloons bursting one by one. It is a celebration of his marriage anniversary. Party is on. Balloons bursting. Back ground music takes over.

In the above scene horse hoofing symbolically expresses the feelings of his loneliness. Absence of music has increased the effect of his depression and loneliness. He is floating in his thoughts without knowing which way his life will take him. Birds chirping, dog barks and sound of a grinding mill coming from a distance create a perfect ambience of a village life. The length of cart running shots have been deliberately kept longer to establish a slow moving life in countryside. When he gets down from the cart Dayal looks at his house in a pan shot with fade in of soft and soothing music conveying his satisfaction and peace of mind that takes him to dawn memory lane.

When he enters in to the house, doors crackling and pigeons fluttering with spider's net around establish the house which is not opened for years and also symbolically reflects his own shattered life. This is conveyed without the use of dialogues or monologues. He looks at the dusty frame of a family photograph placed in a corner, taken on the occasion of his golden marriage anniversary reminding him of his past when they all were so happy in the family. The dust on the photo frame again symbolizes the tragedy of his life. The bursting of balloons is a reminder of his yester years. The flash back with a party creates an emotional contrast with the earlier scene. This gives an emotional relief to the viewers who were carried away by Dayal's agony. In this scene the back ground music is not used as a filler but to create special atmosphere and convey a particular mood whether it is when Dayal looks at his house after long years or when they all were a happy family which is conveyed in a party scene in which all his family members are seen celebrating the occasion together and the music appropriates the mood. In fact the music in the film has been used as a character so it does not seems to be forced or filling the gaps in the sound track. This is a reason that whenever back ground music is heard it touches the core of the heart. In many places there is no sound except the general effects for the ambience.

When we talk of editing in the film it is observed that editing was completely preplanned at the time of writing the screenplay and every sound used was meticulously thought of in advance however the Editor created the suitable pace by lengthening the duration of the shots to show Dayal's despair and loneliness. If the Editor would have cut the film faster the entire mood and effect of the scene would have been spoiled.

The use of sound effects is mostly for ambience and support the mood of the film rather than to fill the gaps.

Television Musicals:

The main difference between musical performances in films and television is that in films it is preplanned, predefined and pre recorded before the shoot which is played back for shooting but in television it is either a live recording or a live show where Director has little control except controlling multi-camera set up and visual mixing by editing on the spot. There can be no interruption in between the performances unlike in films where performance and action is divided in too many shots and filmed under the direction of a choreographer.

While a live performance is edited on the spot in a vision mixing console, it is deviated from many fundamental rules of editing which have been in vogue for long time. It is due to multiple cameras at work simultaneously and the Producer has to choose one among many while the rest continue to record incessantly. All the cameras may not be placed as per these rules since they capture the event from all possible angles. Therefore the Director may choose a shot that does not confirm the basic principles of film editing. There is no predefined and preplanned editing for a live recording. Now days some fiction series are also shot with multiple cameras' set up where major part of the series is shot on a regular set. Outdoor scenes are shot by other directorial units. This deviation from fundamental principles of editing may also cause some visual jerks but they don't create any psychological disturbance as the viewers attention is on the performance so they tend to ignore any minor technical flaws. This editorial freedom can be perceived as an advantage for the medium or a disadvantage for attaining technical perfection

Mystery sequences:

Comedy, action, music are the basic ingredients for entertainment in a fiction film. Similarly the suspense has also been an important entertaining feed for a class of audience. Later the mystery films too attained the status of another 'genre' and became very popular with the growing number of dedicated viewers for them. These films include crimes and investigation, murder mysteries, paranormal activities, scare and fear etc. while writing these films care has to be taken to ensure uninterrupted interest and anxiety from the beginning to end. Editor too has many opportunities with his sense of timing and creative vision to ensure that audience is not deviated even for a moment and suspense keep them glued to their seats. Unlike the dialogue and emotional scenes, every shot can either decrease or increase its impact to the breath taking extent with its proper timing and placement. It is the sole discretion of the Editor to decide how much and where a shot has to be used.

Sound effects, back ground music also play an important role apart from editing. It is a coordinated decision of the Director and the Editor jointly. The use of close ups, length of shots and repetitions, properties used in the scene and special lighting effects and shadows also contribute largely to create suspense and interest in the film. The neutral shots used in a scene can give a different meaning in the situation. Generally shots are extended to deepen the mystery but while extending a shot caution to be practiced to ensure that length should not be that much which could reduce the effect of the scene. The suspense should be fluctuating instead of it being linear so the mystery should not be solved prematurely but should peel off its layers one by one. This keeps the audience on their toes balancing their mental stress and excitement, anxiety for a longer duration. In Suspense films viewers should never be allowed to divert their attention elsewhere.

Film- Baazigar

Location-Exterior, Day

Characters: Ajay, Seema

1. **C.U. Ajay talks on a public telephone**
   Ajay-Seema, Try to understand my compulsions. You know well that I have no status or a position to face your father.
2. **C.U. Seema cries on phone other side.**
   Seema- I don't know. If you cannot talk to Daddy then I will tell him everything about you and convince him.
3. **C.U. Same as 1. Ajay. On Phone.**
   Ajay- But Seema....
4. **Same as 2. Seema**
   Seema- Ajay, we have only a weak with us...
5. **Same as 1. Ajay. Seema's voice continue.**
   ...Daddy has fixed my engagement next week.
   Ajay- Ok. Seema, meet me tomorrow. I will find some way out.
6. **Same as 2. Seema**
7. **Same as 1.Ajay keeps the phone back.**

Cut to..

Scene-Garden, Exterior, Day.

8. **C.U. Seema is crying**
9. **M.C.S. Ajay turns to the camera and moves forward**
   Ajay- Seema, You marry where your Daddy wants.
10. **M.C.S. Seema Turns to camera and stands up. Intercut**.
11. **C.U. Seema is shocked**
    Seema- what are you saying?
12. **C.U. Ajay.**
    Ajay- I thought a lot about it. There is no other way.
    Seema-Ajay, I dont want a way. I want a destination. And my destination is you. I cannot live without you
    Ajay- then we have only one solution which can unite us forever.
13. **M.C.S. Seema is behind Ajay. He turns to her.**
    Seema- What?
14. **M.C.S. Seema is behind Ajay. He turns to her.**
    Ajay- suicide.
15. **C.U.o/s. Seema to camera**
    Seema- Suicide?
16. **C.U. o/s. Ajay to camera**.
    Ajay-Do you agree?
17. **C.U.o/s as IN 16.Seema**
    Seema- if death is the way out of our love, I am ready to die happily
18. **E.C.U. a letter enters in the frame where it is written that... In the same frame another letter comes**
    Ajay- I, Ajay, write in full consciousness
    Seema- I Seema write in full consciousness ...

Ajay-that without pressure from anyone in frustration with life...

Seema - that without pressure from any one in frustration with life...

19. **Ajay and Seema sit under a tree.**

    Ajay- is committing suicide.

    Seema- is committing suicide.

    Ajay- and nobody are responsible for it.

    Seema- and nobody are responsible for it.

20. **E.C.U. Ajay and Seema sign on the letter.**

    Ajay- sign in here. Seema signs on the paper.

21. **M.C.S. Ajay laughs and moves out of the frame.**

    Ajay-shit...

22. **Long shot. Ajay comes to the camera and tears off the note signed by him.. Seema stands behind**.

    Seema- what happened?

    Ajay- because you are passed with hundred percent marks.

    Seema- Hundred percent marks?

23. **C.U. zoom out. Ajay walks to Seema**

    Ajay- Because I was testing you. For your love and for your trust on me.

24. **M.I.S. Ajay throws away his note.**

    Seema- then why this suicide note?

25. **M.L.S. Ajay comes to camera. Seema stands behind him.**

    Ajay- only cowards commit suicide and Ajay is not so weak that he will lose the battle of life so easily...

26. **C.S. o/s. Ajay.**

    Ajay-...we will have court marriage tomorrow. Come to marriage registrar's office at one. I will wait for you there. Now are you happy?

27. **C.S. o/s. Seema smiles.**
28. **C.U. Ajay looks at her.**
29. **C.U. Seema moves out of frame laughing.**
30. **C.S. Ajay looks at her going away.**

Cut to-

Scene, Terrace, night.

31. **C.S. Trolley. Ajay moves forward and see Seema who looks away. Romantic duet song.**

.

32. **C.S. Zoom. Seema takes out her Wedding necklace from her drawer. And looks at it with smile.**

Cut to-

Sun rise, Next Day. Marriage Registrar's office.

33. **Long Shot. Exterior of a building. Marriage Registrar's office.**
34. **C.S. Ajay and Seema looks at the board. It is lunch time.**

    Seema complains to Ajay. From One to two. See it is lunch time.

    Ajay- How did I know that in every office people feel hungry only between one and two?

    Seema- Now what do we do for half an hour? If somebody notices us...

    Ajay- can't do anything. Let them take lunch and let's too go and have air.

Cut to-

Terrace, Day.

35. **Extreme long shot. Top angle from the building. We see everything tiny. Seema looks down.**
Seema- Oh my God. People look like ants from here.

36. **M.L.S.Seema stands with her back to camera. Building is in the back ground. Seema turns back scared and touches her chest.**

37. **C.S. Ajay cleans his specks**

38. **C.U.Low angle.Seema.**

39. **Same as shot 38 Ajay**
Seema-Ajay. Our wedding is so unique.. There is no procession, no band... no dance.
Seema-Ajay, tell me. What is that gift a husband gives to his wife on their first night?

40. **M.S. Ajay scratches his head.**

41. **M.L.S.Seema comes to Ajay.**

42. **Ajay looks at her. When wedding necklace comes in to frame.**
Seema... I knew, you will forget. No problem. I have brought it.

43. **M.S. profile of both.**

44. **C.U.** Ajay- let's see what it is.? Ajay opens the locket and finds photos of them on each side. It is very beautiful as you are.

45. **Long shot. They stand on the edge of the terrace and talk holding each other. Ajay lifts Seema and makes her sit on the wall.**
Seema- Oh.

Ajay- Do you know Seema. I want to take you to the heights of the sky like this.

46. **C.U.o/s. Seema.is scared**.
Seema- what are you doing? I have vertigo. I see circles when I look down. Please take me down.

47. **C.U.Ajay.**
 Ajay- when you have held my hand then why are you scared.

48. **Same as48. Seema**

49. **Same as 49 Ajay.**
Ajay--I am mad to take you away from your world after marriage.

50. **Same as 48. Seema.**
Seema- Every girl has to build her new world after marriage…

51. **C.U. Ajay removes his specks and sits down. He looks at her feet.**
Ajay-…And walking on these beautiful feet she is relieved from all her ties and gets freedom from them forever…

52. **C.S. Low angle. Seema looks down.**

53. **M.C.S. o/s. Top angle. Ajay lifts her feet up saying-**
Ajay-…I am giving you freedom. Forgive me Seema.

54. **C.S. Seema falls down on her back. She shrieks.**

55. **C.S. Ajay gets up and lifts her feet.**

56. **C.S. Seema rolls and falls back from the building.**

57. **Long shot. Seema falling down**

58. **Long shot. Top angle.Seema falling down.**

59. **C.S. Seema falls on the ground dead.**

One of the trend setters in Mystery films of Bollywood, which earlier depended on clichés like scary music, horrifying visuals, surprises and shocks, the horrible looking antagonists, needle of suspicion shifting from one character to another, shadow play etc. and a great hit of its time Abbas-Mustaan's 'Baazigar' not only catapulted its antagonist lead actor Shahrukh Khan to become a super star but also established that an 'antagonist' could be a lead character of a film, the concept which was taboo years back. The antagonist who is a lead character of the film is a serial killer. He hooks beautiful girls in to his love charm to win their blind trust and kills them later. In the above scene of the film' Baazigar' Ajay the serial killer traps Seema in to his love web. The scenes provide a chronological development of his evil design to kill her without getting legally involved in the murder. From the beginning knowing well about his modus-operandi the unsuspecting audience enjoys their romantic relationship giving him benefit of doubt without any adverse presumptions to follow. Their intense love gains support of the viewers who keenly wait for them to get married. Their reaching to Registrar's office for court marriage signals their unfailing love for each other. Ajay dictating a suicide note for them has another twist when he confesses that it was just a prank to test her trust. Nobody could suspect anything wrong in his actions as such pranks are very common between a boy and a girl. Even in the last act when he lifts her feet and compliments her beauty, no one had inkling that something wrong would happen till Seema is finally pushed to death from the edge of the terrace by Ajay. A pure romantic scene followed by a duet song in between takes the audience to a completely different route. While people are aware of Ajay's intentions for some mischief it was difficult for them to anticipate that he would kill her. It is more or less a writer and Director's scene and Editor's role in editing is limited to the timing and pace of cutting only. There is nothing an Editor can do more than what is routinely required in a normal dialogue sequence.

Montage:

The 'montage' is created in different references and contexts by joining number of disconnected shots. Russian film makers called it 'Creative editing.' However many others did not agree with this interpretation. Fast cut shots juxtaposed by a direct cut, a dissolve, a wipe were also called 'Montage.' a scenic transition, time lapse, change in location and transition from one scene to another can be shown by a montage. This series of visuals create an individual or group effect. In a montage sequence various shots picked up from different scenes are juxtaposed to provide a recap or preamp of events to the viewers in a short time. This technique is commonly used in television series. In modern montage sequences smaller shots are taken from real events and action to summarize the meaning of the content. In fiction films montage facilitates to jump in the story line and period where the shots may not serve any emotional or dramatic purpose or it is not necessary to dramatize it but reflect some development in the content or storyline. Therefore the montages carry forward a phase of the story in short. For example a child witnesses a murder and he describes it in detail to his mother. The child is scared. This chronological narration of murder is very important to move the story forward but it is not necessary to narrate the event in its full length and duration as it may consume lot of filmic time and duration and still may not be effective and interesting besides lacking emotional involvement of viewers in the scene. Without this scene it will be difficult to understand the link which the scene provides in the development of the story. A Montage containing series of shots from this event will be enough to serve the purpose effectively. Most of the Montages don't have any emotional effect but they are very important in storytelling. There is normally no pre planning of a montage sequence. If necessary the writer provides a gist of the montage in few words like' Police investigating a crime.'

It is the responsibility of an Editor to work on a montage sequence after the completion of the shooting. Shots are selected as advised by the writer in the script. These shots can be selected from the shot material, stock, unused material or shots from other films available in the library, still photographs etc. that's why most of the montage sequences are edited after the completion of entire editing of the film. At this stage Editor is aware of the material available with him so rest of it will be procured by him from other sources as mentioned. In a fast paced montage the length of the shots should be such that it is registered by the viewers. Efforts should be to select shots which are scenic and eye-catching. Sometimes unused retakes, NGs or left over material are also useful in making a Montage.

Montages present a new idea instead of a direct narration of a story. They fill up the gaps and intervals in the story so it should not be longer than required otherwise it will disturb the mood and the pace of the film and thus will no longer serve its purpose. Another important factor of a montage is that it should be a single unit of visuals which should be unified by suitable back ground music. Dialogues should never be used in a montage sequence as they may create confusion. If at all it is necessary to have a dialogue montage, the dialogues should be linked properly to avoid confusion. Normally such dialogue montages are part of flash back.

It is clear that Montage is used mainly for experimental purpose therefore their use should be minimal only wherever it is required and necessary. Viewers accept a montage as a distant observer that takes him away from the main content for a while. He has his own view point on a montage which may not match with his emotions. Repeated use of montage reduces the dramatic impact of pre defined montage sequences as given in the script however some time intelligent montage work as a miracle to have a better dramatic and emotional effect on the viewers.

*****

CUT-6

Film Editing: Non Fiction

The creativity and merit of a Director in fiction film is proved by his story telling, guidance to actors for effective performance and dialogue delivery, presentation of scenes, shot composition, camera movements, proper sets and settings, music etc. He has a big team of experts to support and realize his creative pursuits that include a writer, assistant directors, cameraman, art director, lyrics writer and music director, costume designer, recordist, editor and actors. Against this non- fiction films are made in completely different surface where the seed is only an 'Idea'. This 'idea' is based on Director's individual thinking, imagination, beliefs and ideology. He has a faint blue print of what he wants to do limited to his own psychological boundaries. This blue print cannot be transformed in to a detailed and neither final script nor can the same be translated in to visuals on the screen as non -fiction films are based on reality and the 'reality' changes as per time, place, director's individual perception and viewpoints. It is not necessary for two different individuals to think alike on a similar situation. Their point of view and interpretation may be different. Their interpretation depends on their upbringing, their social and economical conditions, their culture and education, their family and social traditions and limitations etc. that's why an idea is interpreted, thought of and presented differently by different people. It would not be wrong to say that non- fiction films are more 'individualistic' than fiction films so it is not necessary that others have to agree with them.

The non- fiction has following categories of films-

1. **Documentary films**
2. **News Films**
3. **Experimental documentary**
4. **Educational films**
5. **Docu-drama**
6. **Compilation films**
7. **Promotional films**
8. **Animation films**

Documentary films:

Opposite to fiction, documentary films are made on different concept, perspective, ideology and criterion. In documentary no idea can be untouched and unseen on which a film cannot be made however a subject which has so far not been filmed is the most ideal one for a Documentary. The subjects can be derived from the insensitivity of a society, community or a class over an issue social, political, economical, traditional, beliefs and superstitions etc. which can compel a film maker to passionately ponder about it with an urge to sensitize the people and society at large. It is said that the entire format of a documentary film is prepared only after the shooting on editing table even though the importance of technical knowledge of a film maker on concept development, shot taking, use of sound and narration cannot be undermined. It will not be proper to deny that most of the documentary films are made on editing table due to their vast and research oriented subjects that make it almost impossible to predefine a script on paper as more and more facts, figures and information keep tumbling out of the blue during the production of the film. It is not necessary that every bit of information received and revealed is important for the film but the possibility of its importance at a later stage cannot be over ruled. This gives a distinct identity to documentary film compared to fiction films therefore the production procedure, style and technique is also different than that of a fiction film. The difference between a fiction and a documentary gets blurred when a fiction film based on the real issues and situations are dramatized which looks very real and not concocted. Such films can be easily categorized as a 'Docu-drama' which will be discussed in the coming paragraphs.

The absence of a plot in documentary films is as beneficial to a filmmaker as it is harmful. A story in fiction films keep its viewers tied up on their seats in till film ends. Some lacunas are taken care of by the presence and the performance of stars and presentation but the same privilege is not available to a documentary film maker however documentary makers enjoy more creative freedom than their counterparts in fiction films. A theme is the takeoff point in a documentary film which is developed by a documentary maker based on his individual perception and interpretation. He does not limit himself to the boundaries of a story. The success of a documentary depends upon its 'treatment' of the subject and not on its entertainment value. Cinematography and editing are the two pullers for the quality of a documentary. In the absence of a rigid screen play, a documentary director can edit the film the way he feels the best. He does not have to rely on a narrative (dialogue track), chronology of the scenes or shots etc. He can change the chronological order of his shots and scenes whenever he requires doing it. He is free to interpret the content as per his view point. This creative freedom and interpretation of a subject makes a documentary interesting and purposeful. It is more so good when the viewpoints of the Director and the viewers become similar.

The cost of a documentary film is much less than that of a fiction film which limits the number of crew members to few selected one. The crew of a documentary film consists of a Director, a cameraman, a recordist and an editor with minimum number of assistants. Since the documentary films are made by a Director based on his individual perception and interpretation of an issue, it is not proper to have an independent script writer and an Editor. The difference in their perception, interpretation and ideology will come in conflict at various stages and will be confusing therefore the Director should bear the responsibility of unifying the film. A successful documentary film maker unlike a fiction director must have the knowledge of writing, direction and editing to reflect his ideology in the film. The Director should work out a probable editing plan before the shooting to help him to do the research and script on the subject accordingly. If the script of a documentary is written by another person, the Director would be reduced only to the role of a translator where his own individuality will be absent. In this case it will also be difficult for him to understand and reflect the perception of another person. The end result of the same will be utter confusion and waste of resources so for his own individuality Director should never shy away from writing and doing research of his documentary film.

Documentary Film: Infiltrators.

Director- Urmi Chakroborty

1. Long shot, Exterior, Mumbai VT. Station.
2. M.C.S. Display board of central Railway.
   'In Maharashtra the controversy is acute. The Government has raised the issue of infiltrators.'
3. Long shot, Night. A police jeep moves to Migrants' locality.
4. C.S. wheels of a moving train.
5. C.S. News paper reports about deportation of Bangladeshi migrants-
   'Between1985 and 1991 the govt. could deport only merely 4246 of the suspected over a lakh Bangladeshi. But in1994the controversy surfaced once again'
6. Long Shot. Secretariat building-
   'The Govt. of Maharashtra responded to the circular of election commission of India.'
7. C.S. camera in the running train. We see shanties on both sides of the train. Women wash utensils on the road. A Police inspector searches something.
8. M.L.S.A police jeep is coming
9. Long shot. Shanties on both sides. Police jeep enters.-

'In response to the circular the state cabinet had approved a list of areas spread over44 of the 72 Police station and chose the police instead of revenue department to conduct the verification.'

10. C.S. Police jeep stops in a lane
11. C.S. Three bare bodied boys play cards. They run when they see Police. They are all Bangladeshi migrants.
12. Long shot. Police chase them.
13. M.C.S. People come out of their houses to see the police.

The controversy assumed serious political proportions. Maharashtra govt. released a list of 45000 people from voter list.-

14. M.C.S. People come out of their houses to see the police.
15. Long shot. Police jeep stationed. The constables bring the boys who ran away seeing the police. They are pushed in the jeep.
16. C.S. Paper clips spread on the table.
'The Bangladeshis living in shanties are exploited by ISI agents.
Some of the Bangladeshis were pushed in by Pakistan across the line of control in to the Jammu region.'
17. C.U. Photo of Osama bin Laden.
18. C.U. Photo of a Bangladeshi

'The migrants could become a source for the tailor made army of ISI to formant the trouble in the country.'

Urmi Chakravorty's documentary on illegal migration from Bangladesh' Infiltrators' details about the depth of the problems caused by illegal migrants from Bangladesh since after Bangladesh war of 1971. In fact these are the people who have no land of their own either in Bangladesh or in India. They belonged to 'No men's land.' Suffered from discrimination and survival issues they had entered in to India from its Porous border with Bangladesh. The film was a challenge for its Editor who had to line up completely disconnected material and give a shape which communicated in depth of the issue. Most of the material shot had no continuity and a meaning since the issue was social as well as political one, the commentary writer had to step in to explain the problem faced by India which became an economic burden to many adjoining states. The selection of the right shots and their placement was not an easy task but dedication of the Editor and his creativity worked well to shape up the film. Generally Documentary films are treated inferior to a fiction film but it is not so. It is much more difficult to make a Documentary film that communicates than a fiction mainly due to the fact that a documentary is made out of nothing in hand whether it a script or finance, both are not available in this case.

News Films:

As the name suggests News Films which are commonly known as 'News Reels' are based on day to day events and happenings in our society and the nation. Though slightly different in nature news films can be divided in to two categories- **1. News Reels and 2. Reportage.**

News reels:

We are always curious to know about the happenings around us. The same has become a journalist's delight who totter around the globe to gather information and feed our starving minds. The journalists deliver news as spicy as possible with their own perception and interpretation. Sometimes they dig news out of a mole hill and spice them to be the next headline. But is it possible to spice up news to be interesting? May not be so. The interest in any news depends on the readers/viewers individual liking and disliking. Some may like political affairs and others may like sports news, some may be interested in Arts and few others may be passionate about films, some are sensitive to social issues including domestic one and some enjoy news on crime and investigation, businessmen will be more interested in business news and fluctuation in stock markets around the world. That's why in a news paper there is something for everyone's appetite. Similarly a News reel can be a combination of multiple news items pertaining to Politics, social issues, development, sports, business, international affairs etc. in a film catering to various interest groups.

Now a very pertinent question comes up whether a journalistic piece published in a news paper or a magazine will make an interesting newsreel on film, the answer is same as above, it may not be so. The news reels shot on a celluloid are a visual presentation of a news items which has to see the light on the screen within a limited time period. Now with television taking over this role of disseminating news in visual format in short, interesting and balanced manners and above all at the earliest before any other channel breaks the same news and makes it a headline for the day. To be the first among all the television the news correspondents go for news hunt 24x7. It is not necessary that every piece of news can be an interesting Headline similarly every interesting news may not be an interesting news film. The speech of a popular leader will not be interesting for a News reel because people have already read or heard about it earlier. Readers like the speech in a news paper because they read it there for first time. It would be fresh news for them. The news reels are devoid of such privilege of being fresh as by the time a news film is made it becomes stale. The modern television has technically evolved, equipped and innovated to tackle this problem. The direct and live telecast of the event and talk shows from the studio and the location, breaking news by the newscaster etc. are few of such innovations. It has made production and exhibition of News films more difficult and challenging. The news on television and Radio are produced and broadcast in a similar procedure however the production and exhibition of news films is a completely different ballgame.

The content in a News film should be relevant to the main news. The background, personalities involved, geographical regions and reasons, social relevance and the social and national impact of the news must be carefully analyzed to make it relevant and interesting to this category of people. The news items picked up for the purpose should be such that they don't get stale very soon. An international event or a speech by a popular leader attract immediate attention but other details of the leader like his mannerism, his speaking style, his personality, events location etc are not properly informed in a news paper which can be easily filmed and shown in a news film so these factors should be given prominence.

News Reel: The last journey of Mahatma Gandhi

1. L.s. Gandhi's house- Back ground Music. Prayer chanting-

    Raghu pati raghav raja ram....

2. M.S. Gandhi sitting on a cushion is busy writing letters. A man enters. Gandhi gives him the piece of paper and gives some instructions.

3. 3. L.S. camera is inside the house. Outer door opens indicating that Gandhi will go out.

4. L.S. Gandhi climbs down the stairs with his associates. Frame freezes when he is on the last step. Music fades out.Sound of three bullets fired.

5. C.U. Gandhi's dead body. Zoom to show three bullet marks. (dissolve)

6. C.U. Photo of Pandit Nehru-

7. The dark and blank frame .Pt. Jawahar Lal Nehru expressed the sentiments of thousands and millions of people-**'The light has gone from our life and there is dark everywhere around.'**

8. L.S.   Ocean   of   people   to   give   tribute   to Gandhi.

9. L.S. Gandhi's Last view.

10. L.S. Crowd of millions.

11. Tracking shot. Top angle. On the road sides people view Gandhi with folded hands.

12. Pan shot of the crowd near India gate.

13. L.s. Gandhi's procession moves forward slowly amid thousands thronging around.

14. E.L.S. crowd.

15. M.S. Lord Mount Baton moves with the procession.

16. C.U. Gandhi on the flower bed.

17. M.L.S. Nehru and Mount Baton stand together.

18. M.S. funeral pyre is burning.

It is a matter of fact coverage on Mahatma's last journey which was attended by millions of people coming from around the world to pay their respect to the departed leader who brought freedom for India. Jawahar Lal Nehru's words 'Light has gone from our life' is a reflection of the void the death of Mahatma Gandhi had created. Such coverage besides having immense news value also has archival importance.

Reportage:

Presenting the real and life events interestingly in such a way that they don't lose their natural effect are called 'Reportage'. In reportage the Director only presents the reality and fact but does not give his own opinion , interpretation or decision on the issue. The basic purpose of reportage is to provide in depth factual information about the event without distortion and not to promote or publicize it. it's realistic approach itself makes it interesting so the Director must disseminate the truth and only truth appropriately for example a cricket match, national international competitions, social and cultural events etc.

Ideally Reportage consists of a single in depth story however sometimes there can be more than one in depth coverage in one film like it is in a News Magazine or a periodical. In such cases the combination of different Reports in a film can be aptly called a 'News Magazine' However it should be ensured that no item in the News Magazine is out dated and they should be referred within a specified period.

It may seem that presentation of a Reportage is very simple but it is not so. Suppose a Director covers and presents a cricket match or any event from the view point of the viewers from a fixed place and angle, will that be so interesting? The answer is probably 'No' because while shooting from a fixed angle and distance many interesting elements are missed out which a viewers experiences on the spot. Another point is that the real time (duration) of an event is much more than the filmic time. In a reportage the entire event of few hours is squeezed into few minutes of screen time therefore the main event with all its interesting elements is covered from various angles and distances and edited in such a way that the viewers get a sense of entire happening in a short time. Similarly a Rocket launch from a fixed angle and distance will probably show the entire process of launch but it will be devoid of its other interesting elements and the presentation will be flat therefore preparations, purpose, problems and benefits of launch must be explained for the information of the viewers to build up for the event before the actual launch. This will not only create interest but also curiosity for knowing more about the event and the launch will be its climax. While reporting an event Director should not forget to explain the background, the ambience and the purpose of the event including the people involved in the exercise. In the first example of a cricket match squeezing the duration of the event interestingly is more important while in other example of Rocket launch other detailed information behind the real explosion are also important. In both the example there is need for a director to do a rehearsal but he needs to select the shots and edit the event so interestingly that the message is not lost and originality and reality of the event is maintained.

Reportage: Putin's visit to India.-

1.   An air craft lands on Indian soil.

2. C.U. national flags of India and Russia flutter atop the cars.- Mumbai – 2nd October 2000.

3. M.L.S. President Putin shakes hands with the Indian foreign minister Jaswant singh after alighting from the plane. His associates stand nearby.- President Putin arrived on a four day visit to New Delhi, India. The foreign Minister of India welcomed him at the airport.

4. L.S. President meeting people.- . He also met Russian representatives in Russian Embassy in India.

5. M.S. as in shot 4.

6. Children wave flags of both the countries.

7. The president wave at the children and enters in to his car.

8. Putin's car is running.

9. L.S. Indian President's house.- Tuesday, the 3rd October, 2000

10. President KR Narayanan, Prime Minister Atal Behari Vajpayee and foreign Minister Jaswant Singh wait to welcome president Putin in the president's house.Putin's car stops there. He shakes hands with them after coming out of the car.- The president Putin arrived at the Indian president's house where he met the Indian president Mr. KR Narayanan.

11. L.S. President's riders stand nearby on their horses.

12. Putin meets the prime minister and the foreign minister of India.

13. L.S. national flags of India and Russia atop President's house.

14. L.S. Putin stands on a platform.

15. E.L.S. soldiers of Indian army pay Guard of Honor.- President Putin is Inspecting the Guard of Honor at the president's house.

16. Army and Navy band is played.
17. L.S. Putin walks on Red carpet. On both the sides soldiers from all the three commands stand in attention.
18. M.L.S. as shot 18. Putin walks out of the frame.
19. Zoom in. Putin is meeting people at the president's house.- President Narayanan introduces President Putin to dignitaries.
20. President Narayanan meets Russian representatives being introduced by Putin- President Putin introduces Mr. Narayanan to Russian representatives
21. C.U. Prime Minster Vajpayee.
22. Putin comes to meet press representatives.- Putin also meets press representatives.

It was President's Putin first visit to India therefore people would be more interested to know about his personality, mannerism, his behavior, speech. In this visit his body language was being minutely observed by everyone. One should know that important leaders don't visit a country frequently or repeatedly. We know about them only whatever little we read in newspapers but they have their identity only through visual media. They are very important for archives and historical references. The visits of foreign dignitaries reflect the nature of relationship between two countries which is also reflected in the body language of leaders. Such news films are a visual representation of history for the present generation. They identify these leaders only through news films made on them. For example Gandhi , Martin Luther King, Abraham Lincoln, Gorbachev, Bill Clinton or any other world leaders have got their recognition through news reels. If there would have been no films made on them, their identity would have been shrouded in anonymity. The news about them in print media would have only popularized their names and not their visual identity. In this situation people would have drawn their caricatures as per their imagination as we do with our ancient Gods and Kings. No one knows exactly how they looked like as no one had seen them. This is one of the most important reasons to make news films on important leaders, national or international event and celebrations etc. in an archival format as these news reels create a visual history of a nation therefore it is our profound duty to make news films even if they don't have their presence felt in the din of other media.

Reportage: Curtain Raiser-Asian games 1982 India.

1. 1951. Long shot. (B&W shots)Contingents march in the stadium.- New Delhi. The venue of the first Asian Games held in March 1951. Eleven countries sent 489 competitors to the game.
2. M.L.S. President Dr. Rajendra Prasad is given Guard of honor.
3. M.L.S. Japanese contingent marches.
4. Long shot. The torch bearer comes running.
5. Long shot. The player fires the flame with his torch. Cut to...
6. 1982.The Asian games flame is fired.
7. C.S.. Chinese girls clap.
8. Long shot. A sikh walk fast leading others.
9. C.S.. Pandit Nehru and Indira Gandhi watch the ceremony.
10. L.S. Japanese runs.
11. C.S. a Japanese long throw.
12. M.L.S. Nehru salutes.

13. Long shot. Contingents of all the countries with their national flags.- **More and more countries participated in Asiad. The Asian games move to Manila, Tokyo, Jakarta, Bangkok and Tehran. The 8th Asiad once again stayed at Bangkok.**

14. C.S. clapping.
15. M.L.S. Athletes run.
16. M.L.S. hurdle race.
17. Long shot. People watch games in the stadium. National flags of the countries are seen atop.
18. C.S. A Sikh in Discuss throws.
19. M.L.S. Swimming.
20. M.L.S. Games' flame.
21. C.S. flame.- **The Asian games come to stay at the Olympics of the orient.**

Reportage does not mean that it should only contain the current events but can be a reminder of the past. it can also be a history revisited, it can be a 'curtain Raiser' for an important event or to reconstruct the history for establishing friendly relations between two countries, international contribution in peace process, demographic evolution and systematic development of an area etc. by using historical material. For example a curtain raiser for 9th Asian Games which were held in India in 1982 serves as a reminder of the past Asian game held in the country in 1951 to Indian people and how thereafter Asian games moved to other places before returning back to India. The black and white tone of the film jells very well with the period. A precursor to the main event which was first organized in India was necessary and important for Indian people to be aware of the forthcoming moments of pride. The role of an Editor becomes too important when reconstruction of the past is undertaken. It is he who has to be the Director himself and decide about the type of material he would use for the purpose. It is normal not to engage a Director for making a 'curtain Raiser' if it is to be made from the library material therefore it is the Editor who shoulders the responsibility and proves his creativity.

Some question that why the tempo of an event should be changed when Reportage is made and that too by artificial means? Will it not distort the real effect of the event? There can be two answers in argument of this question. One, in a reportage only important elements and facts of the event are included due to the restriction of filmic time. It is not the purpose to give a 'real time' version of the happening. Second, some of the realistic elements in the real event can increase the ambience' effect while in reportage sometimes these elements have to be recreated by the Director to make it more interesting and for the viewers to associate them with the reality. With the effective use of sound and editing desired emotional effect can be created to make the audience feel as if they have been a part of it. These experiences cannot be felt in an unedited rush print of a reportage as required.

Some producers of reportage enact or stage certain portions of the event to dramatize it. In one of the examples of Pudovkin, he wanted to show an explosion on the screen. In order to make them more effective and strong, he buried some dynamites in the ground and shot them when the dynamites exploded. Though the explosion was very strong, it was weak and lifeless on the screen. After many trials and experimentations he edited a scene where there was no shot from the original explosion. He created artificial clouds and burnt some magnesium intermittently to create light and darkness to show the effects of an explosion. In between he used a stock shot of a river which already had some light and shade effects. Thus he achieved the effect which he visualized. He created an explosion by using only real shot of it. Rests of the shot were thrown to waste bin.

People may have different opinion on recreating of an event. In my views it can be proper but not the ideal one. Recreating a situation or a real event may be absolutely necessary in fiction films but may not be resorted in reportage because the purpose of reportage is to show the reality in a dramatic manner but not artificially dramatized reality. One should use only authentic material in reportage to retain its meaning and truthfulness. Another drawback of recreating the reality is that subconsciously it is the Director's own perception gets reflected in it.

The Reportage presents an event straight and superficially as a journalist writes a piece about an event with all its important points and situation impartially. There is no scope of an analysis or a personal interpretation by the Director in reportage. It can be similar to a 'feature' published in a news paper or a periodical while the analysis may be done by 'others', the writer as whole should be unbiased.

The revolution of television as people believe has undermined the importance of news films which were released in cinema halls. The exhibitors' reluctance to screen them in the theatre for commercial reasons has inflicted a death blow for this genre of documentary films. They also cite another reason for not screening news reels due to their staleness. By the time they arrive into the theatre their content becomes out dated and stale beside a regular revenue loss from the advertisement films which are more popular. They may be right in their contention. It is a fact that with 24 hours' news channels repeating the same news through the day and night not only becomes boring and monotonous but they lose their news worthiness. The channels can also not be blamed for such misadventures with news because they need material for 24x7 telecast and it is always a challenge for them to fill up their time slots therefore whatever news they receive becomes a 'Breaking News' the title which is generally reserved for exceptionally important news items..

The technical procedure involved in film making is another stumbling block in the way for faster dissemination of news in theaters. By this time everything shown in the news reel becomes old and back dated devoid of its surprise elements which nobody is interested to watch. Due to limited time available in theaters, it is not possible to have a detailed description and analysis of a news item. In spite of this draw back news films must continue to be made for historical and archival purposes for future references and use. For example Reportage films made on foreign dignitaries visiting the country are a record of the relationship between two nations. They can be used to promote this relationship to the next level by successive governments. These films also attain historical importance in due course and present chronological development of cooperation between two countries for the information of next generation and leadership. News films also link populace of two nations with their past.

Lacking technical knowledge many people argue in favor and convenience of digital technology without realizing that digital technology has no internationally approved standards for production and preservation of films made on digital format. .No one denies that digital productions are faster and economical and requires less space for preservation compared to celluloid. Those who propagate preservation of films in digital form forget that digital technology keeps changing every day. A film shot to day may not find projectors to screen them after few decades as has happened with video and audio tapes. Therefore one has to keep on updating digital films every now and then with changing technology which is highly impossible. So till there is international standardization of any format, celluloid should not be discarded however films made on digital form can be transferred on celluloid (Direct Inter negative) for preservation.

Experimental films:

Most of the documentary films are known for their thorough research, investigation and analysis. For this quality of documentary films they have been recognized as a 'Genre'. These documentaries present the emotional and realistic elements prominently beyond their superficial approach. Flaherty, Joris Ivan and Basil write became icons for their unique approach. They not only experimented with the contents but also with their cinematic approach. The films made by these directors have been far apart in many ways which are still remembered.

The spontaneity of the presentation in a documentary should not be ignored while making a technical and creative assessment. There is no fixed parameter of continuity which is only a factor while writing a script. Story line for a documentary is only an idea around which the entire film is woven like a spider weaving its web. The details including those which could not be executed are worked out only after the shoot is completed before the editing. Most of the documentaries including experimental films have no shooting script. Even if it is there it is merely suggestive as the purpose is not to write an excellent script but to study, understand and streamline the important points. It is generally a guiding script to carry out the shoots and not to miss out any important points. Director must also shoot extra and miscellaneous material as these extra shots can always be used to establish the location, atmosphere and the ambience. The extra material shot or procured by him does not pertain to any particular scene but for the entire film. It means that if the director feels that something can be used somewhere he should immediately shoot it. Editor too does not have a final draft of the script so he too is helped greatly by the extra shots. While selecting shots out of the extras Editor should be mindful of their emotional appeal and meaning to balance the scenes and their continuity, pace and the rhythm while editing. Editor must take note of the following factors before selecting the shots-

1. Subject matter of every scene.
2. The movement of Images must be compatible to other factors in the scene even if they are not important, should not be ignored.
3. The Tonal value of the scene- colors are an important factor to create the atmosphere. For example, a shot taken during day time may give a feeling of middle of the day and also may represent a 'Pleasant day',

reflection in a shot may represent a dreamy atmosphere, silhouette may inform the coming of the night as clouds may indicate the arrival of rains. Silhouette also indicates instability or a danger warning.

4. Emotional content of the scene.

The cumulative effect of the above factors can be achieved only by proper juxtaposition of the shots that makes the scene interesting and appealing. The Editor should not be carried away by a single factor while selecting the shots but should work to obtain the cumulative effect of them. Robert Flaherty's 'Louisiana story' is one of the best examples of the cumulative effect of the above factors. The film is a story of a village boy's adventures.

Experimental Film- Louisiana story

Director- Robert Flaherty

1. With a slow fade in camera pans on Lotus leaves. Leaves and muddy spots on them are seen as black reflection on the surface of the water. The shades of white clouds on the sky are also reflected on water. Water worms creep on the surface.

2. L.S.A black gray alligator swims in the water. Shades of white clouds are seen again.

3. A bird sits on the lotus leaves and its twigs. Camera tilts up and pans to show the things which were reflected on the surface of the water.

4. The surface of a lily pond, scattered Lotus leaves, and an alligator is creeping slowly on a stem.

5. C.U. reflection of few twigs is seen on Lotus leaves. Dew drops are seen on the leaves.

6. C.U. dew drops on a Lotus leave.

7. M.L.S. A beautiful bird is seen on the branch of a tree.

8. L.S .forest, trunks of trees standing on black water. Shining twigs hang. (This shot is taken from a slowly floating raft. Camera pans to opposite direction that gives a three dimensional effect.)After some time a child appears from the trees peddling his small boat... he vanishes and reappears.

9. Camera moves forward amidst forest and hanging branches.

10. C.U. making of whirlpools on the water by peddling of child.

11. M.C.S. camera on the back of the child. He slowly moves ahead stops in between and looks around.- 'He is Alexander. Napoleon, Ulysses, mermaids. Their hair is green. He says- this water meets with the sea .he has seen the bubbles here many times...

12. C.U. water bubbles disturb small leaves.

13. The boy bends down the hanging branches to make way for himself peddling to move away. - and there come long nosed and red eyed wolves.......to dance in the night.'

14. Forest. The boy looks too small amid the oak trees. He comes peddling towards the camera.

15. C.S. the boy peddles out from left to right of the camera.

16. The sun rays filtering out of the trees create their reflection on the water. The sun rays are seen amid flowing water.

17. The hanging branches make their shadows on the water surface in the sun light.

18. A fish swims a little under the water surface.

19. M.S. The boy bends down a bit more under the hanging branches and moves ahead amid lotus leaves.

20. C.U. The alligator raises his head on the water.

21. M.C.U. The boy looks around holding the boat by peddles but he is not able to find the alligator.

22. In a dark place nothing is seen on the water surface except the reflections of the trees' trunks.

23. M.L.S. The boy moves out of the branches.

24. The boy is seen moving away on his boat.

25. C.U. a serpent comes up on the water and moves away from the camera.

26. M.S. The boy moves towards the camera looks and hears around. He touches the bundle of salt tied on his waist.- 'He can never think of losing his bundle of salt that he carries inside his shirt.'

27. C.U. Bubbles in the water.

28. As in shot 26. The boy peeps inside his shirt.

29. .The boy smiles and peddles to the camera.

Camera tilts up with gradual fade into show many lotus leaves floating, beneath the lotus leaves we see activities of water worms in the invisible water flow. In another shot an alligator creates waves by its slow swim. In the 'movement' analysis we see gradual appearance of slow moving lotus leaves with camera tilting. The slow movement of the alligator is similar to other movements which also indicate the direction of its movement. The water waves of shot 1 are also seen in shot 2. It is a mechanical continuity although the movement is almost invisible but it creates an attractive atmosphere and emotional association.

The reflection of white clouds in the water surface is like silhouette, black muddy spots establish the color continuity. If in one shot there is a shadow of lotus leaves than in other the black color of alligator forms a beautiful and scenic ambience. The golden rays indicate a sunny day. All these factors if not seen in combination lose their significance.

The cinematography, the composition of frames, slow and lazy movements, golden sun rays, reflections and silhouettes create an emotional quotient. Every shot has similarity in movements the story and events have very limited relevance separately but when they are juxtaposed they have a different meaning and relationship.

It is quite difficult for an Editor to select shots keeping above factors in mind as all the shots separately have no meaning. There is no formula or chronology to assemble them so the Editor should keep on experimenting with various permutations and combinations of juxtaposition till he gets the chronology as close to the Director's imagination as possible and then try to bring continuity in the scenes. There is no last word in experimental films therefore if an Editor has knowledge, aptitude, creativity and innovations, it works to his advantage. The Editor of a documentary enjoys more creative freedom than his counterpart in fiction films to decide about the chronology, duration, and length of the shots.

Experimental Film: Child on the chess board

Director- Vijay Chandra

1. .E.C.S. a baby plays with a piece and tries to put some where when camera zooms out to show that she is sitting on a chess board and shifting pieces.
2. C.U. smiling face of the baby dissolves to her family photo.
3. C.U. Baby looks at the mirror. Some special effect of her smile.
4. C.U. baby's photo revolves on the screen.
5. C.U. she picks up the telephone and tries to .talk
6. E.C.U. zoom in to the eyes of the baby.
7. M.C.S. Baby pulls a wooden horse toy and fell it down. She claps with pleasure.
8. E.C.S. smiling face of a boy.
9. Shot as in no.7. Baby claps.
10. C.U. of a lady. In special effect a man waves to her.
11. C.U. Baby swings on the wooden hose.
12. E.C.S. Baby is moving the horse and leaves the frame after some time and returns back. In special effect a circle takes rounds and the baby is seen with in it.
13. C.U. an eye through the Peep hole.
14. C.U. ZOOM. A flower on other side.
15. C.U.C.U. through the peep hole Baby swings the horse toy.
16. M.C.S.A man and a woman look through the microscope.
17. Same as in 15.

18. M.C.S.As in 16. The woman is working on a chemistry lab.
19. Same as in 15. Different images of Baby swinging in 5 holes.
20. C.U. meter is distorted.
21. Same as in 15.
22. C.U. of the baby dissolves to the photo of Eisenstein.
23. C.U. Animated logo of atom bomb.
24. M.C.S. baby's image takes revolves on the screen.
25. L.S. Take off of a Rocket.
26. C.U. Smiling Baby. Animation with toys.
27. M.S. A man hangs in the space.
28. L.S. toys kept in a shelve. A planet hangs above it. Baby pushes it back.
29. C.U. All the planets start shaking.
30. C.U. the word' Ram' and close ups of hand, eyes and lips are superimposed.
31. C.U. of a portrait in the back ground and pass through are the nose, ears and fingers.
32. C.U. as in shot31. But there is a statue of a man instead of the portrait.
33. Same as in shot 31 with the photographs of scientists.
34. C.S. Baby picks up the model of the earth from the cupboard and moves to the camera. The frame freezes. Over it there is a montage of wall clock, dancer, Hitler, Nehru, Kennedy, airplane etc in dissolves.frame defreeze and camera zooms to the model of the earth.
35. C.U. Baby revolves the model on its axis. Zoom to the model.
36. C.U. Baby revolves the earth.
37. C.U. A boy smiles. Dissolve to another boy smiling.

38. C.s. Baby is hammering.
39. C.U. Zoom out. Baby keeps a tripod in a corner.
40. C.S. Baby climbs on the tripod.
41. C.U. Baby's feet are unstable.
42. C.S. Baby throws down the mask of a devil.
43. C.U. Mask falls down.
44. C.S. fearful faces in the back ground emerge one after another with the cut outs of hands, feet, nose, and ears crossing the frame. Animation of India and Pakistan in the back ground.
45. C.U. Baby wears the mask.
46. Same as in 44 with the cartoons.
47. M.C.S. Two horrible faces in the back ground and in the foreground Baby reverse the tripod.
48. Zoom in to the eye of one of the fearful faces
49. C.U. of the devil's mask.
50. C.S. Baby pushes the tripod.
51. C.S. Tripod is shaking.
52. M.C.S. Wall shakes.
53. Same as in 51.
54. M.C.S. Drawing room is shaking.
55. M.L.S. Baby shakes the dressing table.
56. M.L.S. Toys scattered on the ground shake.
57. C.U. Baby shakes the dressing table.
58. Special effect of a revolving circle and a building shakes in the back ground.
59. C, U, Baby looks with surprise.
60. L.S. top angle. Fighter planes on the runway.
61. C.S. Tilt down. Baby shakes the dressing table.
62. Camera follows from face to her hands.
63. M.L.S. A fighter plane passes through.
64. M.L.S. Bombs are dropped from the above.

65. C.U. Baby shrieks.
66. M.L.S. Soldiers run with their guns.
67. M.C.S. canons fire.
68. C.U. Baby shaking the table.
69. M.L.S. a BUILDING CRUMBLES.
70. C.U. Baby shakes the table faster.
71. M.L.S. wall shakes faster.
72. SAME AS 69.
73. M.L.S. Toys shake.
74. Long shot. Baby falls down with the table.
75. Close shot, zoom. Table falls and the glass pieces scattered around.
76. Long shot. Nuclear explosion.
77. The smoke of the bomb moves up in the sky.

Vijay.Chandra's 'Child on the chess board' is one of the finest examples of an experimental film which communicates a dangerous idea in a symbolic manner where there is no use of a narrative or a commentary. The film is a montage of visual supported by Music and sound effects. Every shot in the film is totally disconnected and does not communicate anything individually. While the Director's creative contribution to conceive the film cannot be undermined, it will not be an exaggeration to say that 'Child on the chess board' is an Editor's film. His selection of shots from an arbitrary coverage of thousands of meters is not only proper but their juxtaposition to form and effectively communicate an idea which laid only in Director's imagination. The strongly worded message to the world against playing with nuclear hazards that could jeopardize the existence of humanity should be an eye opener to those who feel happy to research   on dangerous devices. The Baby initially and innocently plays the game of chess as she plays with her toys, swings on her wooden horse, talks on the telephone etc. the chess board is a symbol of human desire to win which inherently starts developing since the childhood. Peeping through the peephole and shots of microscope, laboratory and scientist show people are busy in developing technology and they feel happy about their achievements without realizing about the dangers behind their innovations and inventions. As the baby grows she starts pulling a tripod and dressing table. She wants to go further up and climbs on the tripod which starts shaking under her weight but she is not concerned about impending dangers. The scientific developments lead shaking everything around when war like activities engulf the nations and some fighter planes start dropping bombs. The soldiers rush to defend the mother earth when a nuclear bomb destroys everything instantly. The fall of the dressing table and scattered pieces of the mirror glass reflect shattered humanity and the world. The film is a clear message to those that one should not discover a devil in order to control the world and destroy everything by the push of a button. The editor has not only intelligently juxtaposed the disconnected shots to give them a meaning but the use of sound effects and music has cemented the message which director intended to convey through the film. The co-ordination between the director and the editor has been like water in the milk where both of them try to undo the other to achieve their creative excellence.

Educational films:

During the course of the evolution of the documentary films their utility has been felt in many other areas. The purpose of documentary did not remain confined to personal expressions but extended to serve social causes. Documentaries have proved to be very useful for promotion and extension of education due to a saying that' a moving image is thousand times more effective than a written word.' The visual images are retained deeply in the mind for longer duration. This prompted a spur in the production of Educational films for the development and growth of different sections of the society. Whether the films are made on agricultural production or family planning and welfare, use of machinery or equipments, processes and procedures, manufacturing or class room films based on syllabus.etc. Interesting films have been produced. Television too did not leg behind in this area and started producing and telecasting educational programs covering wide range of subjects from Yoga to astrology, cookery to quiz, religious discourses to talk shows, and medical education to child care etc. these programs meant for various segments are not only educational but also informational. With its easy reach television has proved to be a very potent medium of education prompting the launch of many dedicated educational channels.

The format of an Educational film is drawn at the time of writing the script. Considering the subject matter important points for discussion, analysis and research are decided and included at this stage. The purpose and easy communication of these films gain precedence over the personal views and perception of the Director. He has to work within the parameters set for the film. It is the responsibility, creative merits and imagination of the Director to make a film interesting even if the subject is dull. In educational films there is no scope to analyze any other details not relevant to the subject matter. Therefore all the information given in the film must be authentic and matter of fact. The meticulous research, detailed script and technically excellent shooting make an editor's job easy and limited to the extent of assembly of the shot material as per the script and forming chronology and continuity. Thereafter a commentary writer writes words based on the inherent subject information and assessment to match with the visuals.

In many Educational films it is observed that writer gives live commentary as per the visual actions. Though it is always not improper but is not the ideal way of writing a commentary. There is no meaning in translating the visuals into words. The writer should explain the facts and the information which are hidden and not seen visually. There is no use to talk about what is already seen on the screen. If there is no need to explain the visuals, the same space can be filled up with appropriate back ground music and effects. This makes film more interesting. Another aspect which a writer should remember that he should give explanations or information in the minimum words so that people can have a better grasp of the subject and enjoy the visuals and sounds. Too many words in a limited duration of a scene make it heavy and unsustainable. While more words reduce the visual effect, they are also not remembered for longer time as our memory span is very short. The visuals linger in our memory for longer time. Educationists and educational film makers must take advantage of this theory and work towards creating better visuals with the help of a creative cinematographer.

Educational films must be presented in simple and easy language of communication. Editor may use direct cuts, jump cuts, flash back etc. to dramatize the fiction content but in educational films such types of cutting is completely undesirable.sa it may confuse the viewers and drive away from the main subject defeating the very purpose of an educational film.

It is important to know that Education films have two types-

1. **Instructional/Training films and**
2. **Class room films**

Instructional/Training films:

These films can be defined as those films which contain and explain an action, process and procedure of a subject in simple communication methods. These films are made with a specific purpose and category, class, group or for general viewers to promote a business procedure, functioning, technical and scientific experiments, training and exercise for the development of professional and individual skills. Films made on better yield for agricultural produce, ideal scientific procedures for farming, functioning of a unit in a factory etc. come in instructional category.

The difference in training or a class room film is that of its purpose. The training films help increasing an individual's 'skills', the class room films enhance individual's 'knowledge'. It is similar to the difference between an instructor and a teacher. The class room films deal with various academic and professional subjects, common ideology and thoughts, scientific and technical principles, research and references, analysis etc. 'Logical inference' is very important and basic factor in class room teaching films .They have different editorial problems than action continuity.

While editing a training film Editor should ensure that there is no confusion in the action, process and procedures and presentation of the subject. Therefore the shots pertaining to any process and procedure should be assembled in chronological order. Any deviation in chronology will be confusing the process. If a change in order is necessary then it should be clearly pointed out by a pointer. If there is some continuity problem in a procedure editor can use 'inserts' and 'cutaway' shots so the viewers can understand the change easily. Pan, tilt or wipes can also be used for change and maintaining physical continuity beside the change in location. In training films where live shooting is not possible, still photographs, animation, artificial models or a short statement of the experts can be used. Models can be used to demonstrate the working of a machine, internal parts of the body, process and equipments etc. Many times a big machine or equipment is shown in Long shot from outside and then switch over to close shots of the model of the same for rest of instructions. This does not create any continuity problems for the scene.

Training film: safety in construction

Produced by central labor institute of India this training film 'Safety in construction' caution construction workers about the safety measures they have to observe during their work to save them from unexpected accidents.

1. Two labors are working on a height of a building construction. One of them Pankaj has taken full

precautions in his work while other Shankar is carelessly working.

Pankaj- 'Oh Shankar. You are working so carelessly. See we are on such a height.'

2. C.U. Shankar's feet without safety shoes.
3. M.S. o/s. Pankaj and Shankar talk.
   Pankaj- no shoes, no helmet, no safety belt...'
   Shankar- Pankaj, scared is those who are dead. Let's go. We will meet in the evening.'
4. C.U. Shankar's feet
5. M.S. he is removing a pipe from another pipe.
6. C.U. Shankar's feet slip.
7. M.L.S. He is falling down with the pipe.
8. C.U. Pipe is falling.
9. C.U. Blood soaked hand of Shankar. He is lying on the floor.- **Did you see that this accident has taken place while the worker removed a pipe and fell from the height?**
10. M.S. injured Shankar lies on the floor. Pipe is lying near
11. L.S. Shankar is lying dead with his pipe and sleepers. – **'It is observed that the labor was over confident.'**
12. M.S. An ambulance approaches towards the camera.
13. Tilt up. Pankaj clad with helmet to shoes fixes the hook in a pipe.
14. C.U. Platform with its name and emblem.
15. L.S. labors stand on the platform with railing on all sides.
16. C.U. Of a Toe board and feet on it.
17. L.S. of the labors who have worn all safety devices. We identify the devices with their names and emblem.- 'When you work at a height there has to be

an arrangement of......proper platform......Railing and......and toe board. And safety harness for labors, chug guard with helmet.'

18. In one frame what is right and what is wrong is explained with tick marks.

In this training film, precautions to be taken during the construction work have been underlined in close shots and given prominence by pointers. Hazards of not observing safety measures during the work have been communicated with the blood soaked hand and Shankar's body lying dead. The use of suspense music warns the audience of impending danger and probable accident amidst overconfidence of Shankar. This leaves a long lasting impression of being careless in the minds of the viewers.

The purpose of training films is not only to skill people but also tell them about wrong processes and procedures adopted by untrained and unmindful people and warn them of impending dangers of their actions. It is very important in educational films that no information which could be wrong and unauthenticated should be included. The language of communication should be as simple as possible as it is to be understood by underprivileged or under knowledgeable persons.

Class room films:

Due to variety in target groups class room or teaching films suffer from unlimited variations in their style and format. There is basic difference of continuity between training and class room films. While there is importance for 'action continuity' in training films, in class room films it is to be

'Thought continuity' therefore there is some difference in editing style too. For example in a class room films there can be a montage of physically disconnected actions to underline an idea. Though the shots in a montage may differ in content but they are associated with a common idea or a thought so Editor can only attempt to create physical continuity but it may not be achieved every time. Where it is not possible 'commentary' should be used to explain the idea and smooth the cut. The continuity in class room films is not as big a problem as it seems because of their thought analysis, logical inferences and descriptions, arguments and counter arguments etc. that keeps the viewers involved in the subject matter.

In class room films complexity of subjects and disjointed visual material 'commentary' becomes important. The draft commentary is generally written at the time of script writing which is polished or re-written after the rough cut is ready. Editor matches the commentary with the visuals to relate each of them together. This does not imply that commentary should be loaded from beginning to end and say what is seen on the screen. Such practice of commentary writing deprives the viewers to use their mind. In class room films every point should be explained seriously and clearly. It is possible that people may understand something in fewer words. In this situation extension of an explanation may reduce the pace and make it dry and uninteresting. Similar principle is applied while deciding the length and timing of the shots which should be just as much as required. People may not understand the correct meaning of an unnecessary extended shot and the film may lose its purpose. Therefore the Editor should balance the presentation, time frame and communication of an idea properly. There is every possibility that a class room film becomes dull and slow because most of the subjects are basically dry and lack interesting elements. This dryness can be overcome by the proper use of background music and sound effects.

Docu- drama:

As the name suggests, in a 'Docu- drama' realistic stories and events are dramatized for their re-presentation. A Docu drama is a mix of fiction and non-fiction. The extent of dramatic elements in a Docu drama are not fixed, it can be partial or less than full depending on the objectives and requirements of the film. For example if the film is to be made on a personality the important parts, events and incidents and works of his life can be dramatized. Some people believe that dramatic elements in a nonfiction or a documentary pollute the very concept of non- fiction. According to them a Documentary should be a 'Pure Non- fiction'. But in my view there should not be a tight compartmentalization in non fictions because dramatization makes a presentation interesting. If we can accept dramatization created by effective sound track including Music and effects or by imaginative cutting while editing, why should there be a bar in visual dramatization provided it is assimilated completely with its non-fiction content. Ultimately the purpose of every film is to communicate as interestingly and effectively as to last it longer in viewers mind. However the director of a Docu drama should be careful to see that the dramatization does not become artificial. Some film makers for commercial reasons engage top artists to perform their characters in a Docu- drama. These experiments with stars drive the 'reality' miles away as the stars don't look like and represent the real characters. So one should always avoid artificial settings and known actors in a Docu- drama and as far as possible shoot on actual locations with real characters or those new actors who can be identified with real characters. This will only assimilate fiction with non-fiction otherwise both of them will be like water on the surface of the oil.

One can question whether a complete dramatization of 'reality' be called a Docu- drama. Those in favor of dramatization may agree with it, I may not agree with them as complete dramatization can only be a fiction made realistically because it lacks the style and character of a documentary. The dramatic portion must be preplanned and identified in the beginning while writing the script for better juxtaposition. Editor has to be cautious while editing a Docu drama to ensure that transition from non-fiction to fiction or vice versa is smooth and undisruptive physically or psychologically. The transitions can be direct cuts or dissolves. Dialogues and commentary help in proper transition of the scene so while writing them writer should work to match the content..

Balancing two opposing genres of film making is one of the great challenges for an Editor while working on pace and rhythm of the film. It is possible that documentary and fiction both have their own pace and rhythm due their conflicting styles. This may result in rag tag assembly of fiction and non-fiction. If it is serious problem then its solution is difficult too. The script writer must work on the emotional uniformity of the scenes in both fiction and non- fiction portions while writing the script. In this pursuit prior visualization, commentary, dialogues, editing, transitions, special visual and sound effects and the back ground music are of great help therefore the blue print of the film should be ready before the shoot and editing is undertaken. Since my film school days I was highly inspired by the dramatic elements which are generally used in fiction films from writing to taking of shots and editing to the use of sound effects. This prompted me to use the same in documentary films or Docu- drama. I have no regrets to accept that my documentary films were highly influenced by fiction. It was a memorable experience for me in my own film 'Toote Pankh'.

Docu-drama: Toote Pankh

In the film 'Toote Pankh' after retirement the main protagonist Dayal with his wife shifts to their elder son's home in another city. There He is confronted with the realities of life and he is disappointed by the behavior of his son and daughter in law. He comes across a program on the television on the life of senior citizens and old age homes. After watching the program he is enlightened to decide further course of action.

Scene 1. Dayal's house. Indoor. Evening.

1. Sunset. Dayal is watching television with the family members including his son, daughter in law and grand children.
2. The television anchor introduces the next program.- **'After India got freedom, the industrial development has greatly revolutionized various aspects of our life .that's why our country is emerging as a super power in the group of nations but this industrial revolution has also affected our age old social fabric and joint**

family system. New cities were established but our joint families decimated. The head of the families legged behind to carry the burden of their old age. There was no place for them in the new situations and the new family dispensation. They had place neither in the hearts nor in the homes. Today's program is dedicated to those who carried the burdens of others in their life but have now become a burden themselves.'

3. C.U. of the baby.
4. M.C.U. pan shot from the daughter in law to the son.
5. Zoom to Dayal.
6. C.U. Dayal

Scene 2. Old age Home. Exterior. Day.

1. L.S. Pan showing ext. of old age home
2. Tilt down from the name board of the home to temple.
3. C.U. Deity in the temple.
4. C.U. a man rings temple bell.
5. M.C.U. two old women clapping on the beats.
6. M.S. Low angle, old women on stairs clap on beats.
7. M.S. old men clap.
8. M.S. the priest is singing the prayer
9. M.L.S. people ring bells.
10. C.U. old women.
11. M.L.S. Priest sings prayer.
12. M.L.S. Pan. A man rings the bell along with few women who are clapping on the beats.
13. M.L.S. Low angle of the temple.

14. M.L.S. Top angle. People are clapping on beats. Some bow to deity.
15. A man explains.- L.S. Pan showing ext. of old age home
16. Tilt down from the name board of the home to temple.
17. C.U. Deity in the temple.
18. C.U. a man rings temple bell.
19. M.C.U. two old women clapping on the beats.
20. M.S. Low angle, old women on stairs clap on beats.
21. M.S. old men clap.
22. M.S. the priest is singing the prayer
23. M.L.S. people ring bells.
24. C.U. old women.
25. M.L.S. Priest sings prayer.
26. M.L.S. Pan. A man rings the bell along with few women who are clapping on the beats.
27. M.L.S. Low angle of the temple.
28. M.L.S. Top angle. People are clapping on beats. Some bow to deity.
29. A man explains.- **'In today's busy life, the children are not able to give time and take care of their own parents so they are lonely. They don't get what they need.'**
30. C.U. of baby boy and mother.
31. An old man tells- **Older people have different ways of thinking and their children think differently. This leads to a regular conflict between them.'** sometimes older person's ego is hurt as they are very sensitive**.'**
32. C.U. of Dayal

In this scene the assimilation of fiction and nonfiction has been carried out brilliantly. Television is an important part of our life so a program on 'old age home and senior citizen is not out of context and becomes a character of the film itself. The introduction of the program by the anchor is informative but leaves a long lasting emotional impact on the viewers. Intercutting of the shots in between the television program relates them with the issue as the words spoken in the program somewhere reflect their own problems. It increases the emotional quotient of the dramatization without being separated from main theme. Fiction and non- fiction merge with each other completely. Properly placed reaction shots of family members during the introduction and statements of older people carry the viewers to the basic sentiments of the scene.

The prayer chanted by senior people in the temple is musically raw and out of beats and tune and but realistic. It involves them emotionally and physically. Their activities, participation in the prayer, clapping with their tired hands, helpless and dull eyes reflects their vanished hopes and aspirations. This is perfectly in tune with the character of a documentary. Changing expressions in their faces tell the story of their isolation and loneliness. It increases the dramatic and emotional effects of the scene. This way in 'Toot Pankh' it is fine amalgamation of fiction and non- fiction. I always believed that when a Documentary exposes the reality of people's life why it should also not show the emotions of their life and why their emotions cannot be dramatized to make a documentary interesting. Documentary can never be a tool for personal comments nor should they be without emotions therefore those who believe that there is no place for emotions and drama in a documentary are wrong. Documentary too has the same rights to be interesting as that of a fiction film. For this reasons' Docu- drama attain a place of importance.

Compilation films:

With the combination of letters we make words and seven notes of music create unlimited musical compositions. Similarly with the juxtaposition of unconnected shots innumerous scenes can be created with different commentary. These are the shots which were taken for different purpose and projects but their use in different contexts has a different meaning. With his creative skills a Director compiles, edits and produces a different film using many disconnected shots obtained from different sources. There is no prewritten script or shooting for the film. The material for compilation films comes mainly from archieves, libraries and stock shots from various films shot time to time. The credit for a good compilation film goes to the Director directly for his editorial knowledge and skills. He gives a different meaning to available shots with the help of commentary which is the back bone of compilation films.

The success of a compilation film depends on the interesting and dramatic use of historical facts and importance. It does not mean that whatever is shown in a compilation film is always authentic. The truth prevailing in the stock material can be given different meanings and interpretations with the help of commentary specifically written for different contexts. This gives liberty to the director to interpret a historical fact the way he perceives it. Compilation films cannot be made using the stock material from fiction films except when the compilation film is based on the history of cinema in various regions of the world in which changing patterns of cinema, development of technology, genres, cinematic analysis, films and film makers etc. have to be depicted therefore the use of stock footage from fiction films is very limited. Procurement of relevant material for a compilation film is always a challenging task so whatever is available even if it seems to be irrelevant at the time should be collected by the Editor. The procurement of material may consume lot of money and time of Director and Editor as the material has to be discovered from unknown sources around the world. In the end Editor may find huge amount of material at his disposal so he must begin selecting the relevant material in consultation with the Director and keep the unused one for future. Before embarking on this exercise, the Director should have a fair idea of the probable format of the film once he is aware about the available material.

After a proper selection of the shots Editor should sort them out for the context, cinematic quality and relevance as the shot of a house may indicate poverty or richness. It is a village or a city, it is summer or spring, if it is winter, is it snowy or rain soaked. The shots should be analyzed for their merits and quality and marked with their description on the box or in a log book with their reference numbers. It is also quite difficult for an Editor to juxtapose the shot in proper timing and place as any shift or improper placement may change its meaning and the context. Therefore creative, meaningful and cinematic shots should always be looked for. This is a trial and error' method for an effective compilation film. For example if a shot of a house is shown to establish richness of a person , it will symbolize the rich life style of wealthy but the same shot is shown with artistic references , it will appreciate the design and the gorgeous look of the house. So use of a shot can change the understanding of the viewers about it. Therefore Editor must be extra careful to use any shot with its proper reference and context. Similar type of shots can be used meaningfully in different reference and context with the help of commentary.

After selecting the best shots they should be arranged in proper chronological order. Thereafter enters the commentary writer who after understanding the concept of Director and the Editor, writes commentary for every scene, explains the sense and the meaning of every scene so the viewers understand what they are made to understand. While writing the commentary the writer should know that his words form the sentimental base of the film and the same sentiments have to be displayed by the commentary speaker in his voice by bringing variety in voice tones and intonations. The co-ordination between a writer and the Editor is very essential to achieve technical excellence with proper tempo, timing, continuity and use of proper transition devices like dissolves and fades. Time lapse, change in location, psychological continuity etc, can be guided by the commentary. Interviews, talks and statements also help to interpret the material properly. Similarly the writer may also write the commentary as per the editing pattern prepared by the Editor. The same thing applies to the editing too. Some times Editor may have to change or shift a shot or placement of the scene while matching the commentary. If necessary, Editor must arrange extra shots to accommodate the commentary. How editorial skills can be put to use for a compilation films can be seen in the following example.

Compilation film : Gandhi -An emerging reality

Director- Kuldeep Sinha

Martin Luther King Protest: I have a dream….

1. M.S. Negros is marching forward with play cards in their hands.
2. M.L.S. Pan shot. Leaders are followed by their followers.
3. M.L.S. Pan shot. People are moving ahead.
4. . As in shot 1. Negros marching ahead
5. E.L.S. Washington city.
6. M.L.S. American President Kennedy, Martin Luther King and many others stand nearby. Martin talks- **I am happy to join with you today in what will go down in history as the greatest demonstration for freedom in the history of our nation.**
7. C.U. President Kennedy.
8. M.C.S. TO E.L.S., Zoom. People stand around a fountain. Zoom out White house.
9. M.S. TO L.S. Zoom, Martin Luther King is delivering a speech. People hear him around.-' **Five score years ago, a great American, in whose symbolic shadow we stand today, signed the Emancipation proclamation. This momentous decree came as a great beacon light of hope to millions of Negro slaves who had been seared in the flames of withering injustice. It came as a joyous daybreak to end the long night of their captivity. But one hundred years later, the Negro still is not free. One hundred years later, the life of the Negro is still sadly crippled by the manacles of segregation and the chains**

of discrimination. One hundred years later, the Negro lives on a lonely island of poverty in the midst of a vast ocean of material prosperity.

10. E.L.S. crowd. White house and the forest are seen in the back ground.

11. M.S. people sit and listen to the speech.- **I have a dream that my four little children will one day live in a nation where they will not be judged by the color of their skin but by the content of their character**

12. M.S. Top angle. People are standing. They wear headgears with the words KAACP written on it.- Martin-**' I have a dream that one day this nation will rise up and live out the true meaning of its creed: "We hold these truths to be self-evident, that all men are created equal."**

13. Tilt up. People sitting on chairs and behind them people listen to Martin.- **'With this faith, we will be able to hew out of the mountain of despair a stone of hope. With this faith, we will be able to transform the jangling discords of our nation into a beautiful symphony of brotherhood. With this faith, we will be able to work together, to pray together, to struggle together, to go to jail together, to stand up for freedom together, knowing that we will be free one day.'**

14. L.S. people in an angular position listen to the speech.

15. Low angle. People sit on the front row and in their back some people click photographs.

16. L.S. Martin Luther King is giving speech and people around listen to him.

17. M.S. a group of people on the right listen the speech.

18. M.L.S. people listen the speech- **And this will be the day - - this will be the day when all of God's children will be able to sing with new meaning:**

19. As in shot 10. Camera pans and people clap.

The purpose of the above scene in the film 'Gandhi –An emerging reality' a compilation film by Kuldeep Sinha is to highlight the impact Mahatma Gandhi had made on the leaders of the world around. His policy of non violence had not only influenced the British who were forced to free India after a long bloodless struggle but also lit the flame of non violence elsewhere. Martin Luther King and Nelson Mandela became his devout follower to lead the path of non violence. One can observe many international happenings that had the stamp of Gandhi like breaking of Berlin wall and unification of East and West Germany. The address of Martin Luther King to his protesting supporters promotes non violence. Like Gandhi, Martin Luther King too had a dream for his countryman who reflects in his speech. This coverage is one of the rarest historical one in the world. No one knew while covering this event that it would be used how, when and where and how many times in what reference and context. This coverage has been used in many compilation films in different contexts.

The coordination between writer and the Editor is evident in this scene. With the timing of shots the voice of Martin Luther King has been complemented properly. The synchronization of the voice and visuals provide authenticity to the facts. The voice links the disconnected shots to achieve physical and psychological continuity.

One of the main drawbacks of compilation films is to match the tonal and cinematographic quality of the material procured from various sources. This material is shot on the variety of raw material produced by different companies. This results in the variations in film speed and color sensitivity. Similarly in modern technology there would be difference in the quality of tapes, tonal differences due to various types of camera with variations in pixels and digital projection systems. They produce various results in quality but one cannot deny the importance of content in compilation films however the end quality of the film can also not be ignored therefore while selecting shots Editor should be mindful of uniform photographic quality of the material wherever it is possible. Where there is lot of variations in photographic quality the cameramen should work on color correction before printing. The shots which cannot be corrected should not be selected at the first place and commentary may explain the meaning of such shots.

It is very important to know the historical importance of a compilation film as much as the importance of the material used in the film so there should be no compromise at any level including its research, factual or technical. The Director starts with an idea and thereafter he researches and collects the material from all available resources. Using this material is a challenge for the Editor's skills. Sometimes some rare material makes a film immortal so the editor must use this material creatively to make it an integral part of the content without looking forcefully added one. Commentary can link and integrate such material with the main content easily.

Compilation film : Thus said Indira

Director- Kuldeep Sinha

The last speech Of Indira Gandhi:

1. M.S. Indira Gandhi form the stage addresses a public meeting-'**I am not worried if I am alive or not C.U. Indira Gandhi on the bier but till I breath I will be in the service of nation. Even if I have to die, I can say for sure that every drop of my blood will be for India.'**
2. Pan shot of Public.
3. V/P Indira Gandhi. People sitting in front.
4. C.U. Indira Gandhi on the bier. Zoom out to include Rajiv Gandhi near her

This is one of the gems of historical coverage which contains the last ever speech of the Late Indian Prime Minister Indira Gandhi delivered on 30th October 1984 at a public meeting in Bhubaneswar... Who knew that it would be her last words and she would really not be alive the next day. Her premonition about her death made this speech historically very significant other wise in normal course if she would not have been dead, this speech too would have been forgotten like other ones. Inclusion of this speech is paramount for any film made on Indira's life in future.

Promotional films:

Since its inception cinema has always been a matter of interest for everyone. It became an important medium of entertainment but in due course cinema became a medium of communication and dissemination of information. With this there have been wide spread openings for films for various commercial and promotional purposes. Industrial houses and professional organizations that saw potential for their business abroad needed an attractive presentation about their business for their foreign clients. These business houses and export companies needed to project their Image, activities, objectives, their place in the market and their share holdings, past achievements and future plans, vision of the management etc. to their stake holders and clients. They have to communicate it in shortest possible time. Cinema came to their rescue. These films made for a specific purpose became order of the day and there has been huge demand for 'Promotional films' therefore a new category of non- fiction films came in to existence known as 'Promotional films.' This job today is also under taken by Power point presentation but this presentation cannot be as attractive and interesting as Promotional films.

Promotional films can be divided in to two categories-

1. **Promotional Film.**
2. **Advertisement film.**

Promotional Films:

Promotional documentary films are those which are produced with specific purpose of promoting activities of an organization. The company management first decides about the type of information they would like to present in the film. The objective of promotional films is limited to the promotion to create good will and expand its business base therefore in these films only those information are included which could help boost its 'Rating'. Other information which can adversely affect their share holders, business partners, rival companies and the public are rejected. Once main points of emphasis are zeroed in the script writer puts them in order along with suggestive commentary for explanations of facts and figures. Since the commentary is only suggestive, it can be revised any time later. This is called a 'Draft script' of the project. Only after this Director and other crew members come in to action and plan for the production is worked out. The film is shot exactly as the 'draft script' and thereafter comes the editor.

In Promotional films 'Fact' and 'truth' are given more importance in the content however sometimes some facts and truths are also kept under the carpet or diluted to suit its purpose to save the company from any adverse effect as the main objective of Promotional documentaries is to refurbish the image and reputation of the company. Therefore bitter truths are not given more importance and other favorable points are emphasized. Similarly any achievement or success is exaggerated. The weakness if any of the company is generally not highlighted. It is always beneficial to have a vision statement on the company's activities by the chairman or any other from the top management level to establish company's credibility.

There should be no compromise on technical quality of a promotional film whether it is cinematography or sound recording or editing because a Promotional film is a reflection of the organization. Any qualitative deficiency is treated as its carelessness and weakness that's why most companies reserve an exorbitant budget for these films and engage experienced directors with proven merits. The role of an editor too is very important in these films. Promotional films are generally fast paced compared to other films to accommodate as much information about the company in the least possible time. So editor should keep the shots minimal length and cut them fast. There is not much scope for Long shots in the films except if a location of a factory, railways shipyard etc. is to be established. Where loading or unloading of a goods is to be shown. Editor should be sure that fast cutting is not so fast that dilutes the message. While it is not unusual to exaggerate thing in favor of company, the words chosen for commentary should convey more in minimum to give space for the use of music and sound effects.

The back ground music plays a very important role in making Promotional films interesting. While complementing with the basic sentiments of the film music should try to uplift a scene if any out of its dullness. This is required for involving otherwise generally disinterested viewers. Many of the Editors have a collection of stock music   with them which they keep on using films after films. This not only affects its recording quality but also the music loses its novelty so this practice of using stock music should be avoided in Promotional films and fresh music should be recorded as far as possible.

The management of the organization is enticed to load the film with as much information as they can in their Promotional films which is not effective as it turns a promotional film into a catalogue of the organization. To avoid this situation variety of options available with information machinery and technology must be used like animation or graphics for company's data, Models, still photographs, designs, power point presentation for future plans, moving pictures for production procedures etc. for the visual variety. While using these options pace of the film must remain constant. Sometimes a statement or talk with the chairman may obstruct the natural flow of the film. This can be avoided by editor by splitting the chairman's statement into fragments and overlapping them on the relevant visuals.

Promotional film: Khadi and Village Industries Commission

The film example from the Promotional documentary on 'Khadi and Village Industries Commission' promotes the activities of the institution. Like advertisement films it does not promote a product but the dedication of KVIC to the cause of social service to the people of rural India. KVIC is am autonomous organization of the Indian government which was primarily established to realize the dreams of Mahatma Gandhi for the development and growth of rural society.

Scene one-

1. L.S. Tilt down from sky to the courtyard of a house where many people are busy weaving cloth on looms.
2. M.C.S. two children fall on the heap of cloth.
3. C.U. The supervisor looks at them with anger.
   Supervisor- what have you done...scattered all the material.
4. As in shot 2. A lady the children's mother, lifts them up from the heap.
   Lady-- get up...get up.
5. C.U. The supervisor as in shot 3.
   Supervisor- why don't you take care of them?
6. M.C.S. Mother beats her children.

7. L.S. Trolley. A boy is reading some files on a table. A girl is doing something nearby. The boy gets up to set the children free.

   Girl- why are you beating them, Mamta ben?

   Boy- why don't you send them to school? Often I find them loitering here.

8. M.C.S. Mother and children

   Lady-- How do I send them to school? Their father does not pay their fee.

9. C.S. the boy convinces the lady.

   Boy- you should have told me earlier. You can do so. All the children of our institution staff study in8th, 9th and 11th standard or they are in ITI. They also get scholarship under workers welfare scheme.

10. Some people listen to the boy standing nearby.

    Lady-I don't know anything about it.

11. C.S. the girl too starts talking-

    Girl- Now you know. Go and get your children admitted in school and I will try for their scholarship.

12. L.S. Men and women

13. C.S. A lady removes thread from the loom.

    SceneTwo.

14. L.S.A senior officer is on the stage. A boy works on a spinning wheel.

15. M.C.S. some people stand near the stage.

16. C.S. Of a hand spinning on wheel.

17. C.S. of a hand pushing a button.

18. C.U. the light is on.

19. L.S. all the workers clap.

20. L.S.Tilt up.officer

Officer-Brothers and sisters, you see a miracle on spindle wheel. You see, How fast it works. Now Khadi and village industries commission has manufactured a new type of spinning wheel. With this you can produce electricity while spinning. You can light up your home with this electricity.

21. L.S. Top angel. People clap.
22. L.S. A boy Madhav stands up on the stage.

Madhav-Gandhi ji used to say, Khadi is a mission. Khadi is an employment of millions of unemployed people. It gives them to work with dignity. More over it pays them money and respect. Khadi gives them equal opportunity to grow and be equal.

23. M.L.S. People are clapping

'Khadi and Village Industries commission' is not an institution but an opportunity to underprivileged to learn new skills. It is involved in preserving the traditional past and innovating technology for the future. The innovative spinning wheel which also produces electricity to light up the darkness in the lives of rural folks is an evidence of KVIC's passion for the poor.

Advertisement film:

While a Promotional documentary promotes an organization, company or an institution, the Advertisement film promotes a 'Product' or a 'Service'. There is no limit for a promotional documentary but an Advertisement film should not exceed a minute. Due to crunch of time space in cinema halls and television advertisement film vary from 10 seconds to one minute.

The objective of an advertisement film is to attract consumers to buy their products or services so their production can be increased. Advertisement films are generally made to defeat its rival company's products of similar nature by claiming its better quality. It is a great challenge for advertisement makers to entice its consumers with in few seconds to change their buying decisions instantly in their favor. It is also difficult to inform about the product's finer points so quickly and interestingly therefore director's creative merits become more important. The technique in an advertisement film is not more important than its innovative and effective communication. For example a film to promote the need of insurance by an insurance company is one of the best advertisement films I have come across.

Advertisement Film: Insurance.

1. **The scene opens with the camera placed on top of a hill. Down below a long curved narrow pathway is seen. For some time there is no action on the pathway till a car is seen entering from right. The car stops in the middle of the road and the frame. The driver comes out with an empty can to fill up the water for its engine. He looks around and moves out for water keeping the car door opened. In a short while a loaded truck enters in speed and dash ahead breaking the car's door. The frame is freeze with a caption superimposed- 'Your car needs Insurance.**

In this advertisement film the camera has been static throughout and there is no other movement. The film is entirely unanticipated till the caption appears at the last on a freeze frame. There is no commentary to say anything about the product or the service but it leaves a great impact at the end due to its shock element. The film is unique in its form compared to other advertisement films which talk very high about their products or services. There are no high talks, loud back ground music or fast cutting etc as is seen in advertisement films generally. Driver moving out with water can without closing the car's door is a reflection of his carelessness. When the speeding truck runs over the door communicates that accident may take place anywhere any time that's why 'your car needs insurance' leaves a long lasting impression on viewers mind. This advertisement is considered one of the best in the world for its unique, unpresuming and heart touching approach.

With changing times and technological growth people's thinking have also changed. The films with instant effects instead of long lasting effects have come into existence. Increasing demand for a time slot for advertisement films resulted in decreased duration of films to few seconds. Direct communication has been given preference. Negative advertising too came in vogue to attract more audience. Advertisement films with 'sex and sex symbols' to stimulate the basic instincts of people became more popular. Top film and television stars too started cutting their slice in to the advertising revenue. They found an alluring field to earn quick bucks in promoting a product or branding a company. While Advertisement films started moving away from creativity they improved in technical quality.

Due to their short length Advertisement films have more close shots which convey more and quickly. Most of the shots in advertisement films are disconnected so Editor should not attempt to find action continuity in them. Cutting is faster which is counted in the number of frames and not in footage. It should be remembered that the running speed of a film is 24 frames/ second and for television it is 25 frames/ second which approximately 1.5ft. If the total length of the advertisement film is only about 10 seconds in which about 50 shots have been used than the average length of a shot will not be more than few frames. Selection of these frames is not a cake walk for an editor. By blink of a second many shots move away so editor should select such frames which are instantly communicative and highly effective. No shot selected should be static but moving for apt and instant communication. In advertisement films all the means of communication including commentary, dialogues or captions are utilized repeatedly to hammer out the message in the minds of the viewers. The main points of the product or service too should be harped repeated but in different ways to retain its novelty and effectiveness. Whether it is a scene, sound effect, back ground music, commentary or star presence, they all should make a lasting impression in the minds of the audience.

Repetition of advertisement films by various means of exhibition keeps on reminding people about the product that's why advertisement makers release the them simultaneously on the entire medium for a fixed and limited period and repeat them after some interval.. Before production of an advertisement film is taken up the copy writer who can also be termed as script writer for the film prepares a 'draft copy' detailing the main points of the product. This is approved by the management as per their policy. Thereafter the story board is prepared by the visual designer. It is almost similar to the visual screenplay of the film. This visual script gives a fairly good idea about the proposed film they have in mind. The 'story Board' is assessed by the management on the basis of their policy and creative ideas. Once the story board is approved director and his team moves forward to the next stage of production. Since budget is never an issue with advertisement films director and editor have liberty to take as many extra shots they want. It helps them to have lot of options to use the shots which are the best for the fast pace of the film. The number of shots required in an advertisement film is more as only few frames can be used from each one of them to keep its pace fast.

Advertisement film: A Good beginning

1. Long shot. On the sea side bus stop a boy and a girl wait for the bus. The boy moves near to her. She is chewing something.
2. M.C.S.O/s. Of the girl. Boy faces the camera.
    Boy-Excuse me. Can you give me a bite of your Dairy Milk?
3. L.S.O/s Girl facing the camera
    Girl- Do I know you?
4. Same as no.2.The boy shakes his head
    Boy-No.
5. Same as 3.Girl
    Girl-so?
6. L.S. Boy and the girl talk to each other
    Boy- My mother says...Before doing something good, take some sweet. The work is well done
7. Same as 3. The girl after a pause gives him a piece of Cadbury.

8. M.C.S.OSS. boy accepts the Cadbury.

9. C.S. The girl looks at him and eats Cadbury.

10. M.L.S.o/s. Girl to the camera. She asks the boy.
   Girl- what good you are going to do?

11. C.S.o/s. Boy in profile and the girl with her back to camera.
   Boy-I was thinking to drop you home.

12. Same as 10.The girl shifts her looks from the Cadbury to him blushingly.

13. Same as 12. The boy looks at her.

14. Same as 13. The Girl blushes.

15. Same as 12. The boy smiles. Commentary. **A good beginning'. Let's have some sweet.**

16. Graphic design- **'A good beginning"** with a photo of Cadbury.

There is no parameter for the number of shots and their length to be used in an advertisement film. It all depends on the basic idea, story board, the type of medium cinema, television or any other one, time slot available etc. some advertisements can be based on 'Jingles' and others may be 'Dialogue scenes', some can be animated and others can be created in 'Graphics', some are based on stunts and actions and others are comedy. Some are made for a particular 'Target group', age group, product's consumer and specific places where product is to be promoted. Although editor follows the principles of editing for advertisement films too, he has more freedom to experiment with the material however without deviating from the main purpose of attracting consumers. An ineffective advertisement which cannot leave its positive impact about the product is not only unsuccessful in its purpose but also is a creative failure of the entire team including the Director. The product will linger in the memory only when it strikes instantly on the minds of people. The negative advertising or berating rivals to lure people is not proper at least in the consumer products segment as negative effect can be instant for highlighting the product but not retained in long term.

Social campaign film: Public Provident Fund

1. M.L.S. A name board is seen on the wall. The Host enters in to the room to anchor a quiz program on 'Public Provident Fund. He asks the audience about PPF.Claps.

   Host- Do you know the full form of 15 years' PPF?

2. C.U. A young man replies.

   Young Man- Sir, it is fifteen years' Public Provident Fund.

3. M.L.S. of the host.

   Host- It is a unique scheme

4. C.U. A senior PPF officer talks to the camera.

   Officer- Because the interest earned on PPF is completely tax free. Deposit is exempted from your Property or wealth tax too.

5. M.L.S. of the host.

   Host-Do you know how much money you can accumulate in fifteen years?

6. L.S. A lady home maker replies while cutting vegetables.

   Lady-From one hundred to sixty thousand rupees per year at a time or in installments

7. C.U. of a Doctor talks to the camera.

   Doctor- if you invest in 15 year PPF you get tax rebate under 80C.

8. M.L.S. Host asks another question.

   Host- what are the three important benefits of PPF?

9. M.L.S. A lawyer in his office talks.

   Lawyer-The date on your cheque is the date of your PPF account. Provisions of partial withdrawal after two years and Deposits have no court jurisdiction

10. M.L.S. of the host.

    Host- yes, you are right .There are many benefits in investing in 15 years PPF.

11. Caption-'**Invest today-15 year Public Provident fund scheme.**

A simple and effective social campaign film to motivate people to opt for savings in PPF is not only uniquely conceived on the format of a quiz program which itself generates curiosity among the participants. The quiz program wisely involves PPF officials as well as public. While officials answer about the scheme, intercutting statements with public including a young man, lady home maker, A lawyer and a doctor in between acknowledges the fact that people are not only aware about and appreciate 15 year PPF scheme but also recommend everyone to opt for it as it has lot of benefits stored in it for the people. Like an Advertisement film the importance of a social campaign cannot be ignored as government and corporate responsibility towards society. The purpose of a social campaign film is to inform, inspire and motivate people to be part of social initiatives undertaken by the authorities.

Documentary and the sound:

People have difference of opinion on the use of sounds in documentary films. The pioneer film maker Basil Wright of 'The song of Ceylon' favors use of symbolic or expressive or communicative sound track while few others feel it proper to have 'actual sounds' however most of the film makers prefer 'realistic track ' as ideal one. According to this school of thoughts there are limited opportunities to use; experimental sounds' in fiction films but in documentary films due to their disconnected character it is always not possible to use neither actual sounds nor it is desired. The inherent sense and meaning of disconnected visuals can be supplemented by a suitable sound track which is not only effective but also reflective of Director's creativity. In one of the scenes of the film 'The plough that broke the planes' by Pare Lorentz, farmers are shown ploughing the fields. The marching of soldiers in the background is complemented with the commentary as if it is a war field. By the use of marching effects the film maker wants to say that while the soldiers are fighting on the borders the farmers plough their fields so both are doing a service to the country. Use of such symbolic sounds is rare in fiction films but is quite common in non fiction which has its long lasting impact and appeal. Some film makers are very obsessed with experimental sounds sometimes due to economical reasons. The documentary films are generally made with shoe string budget where it may not be possible to hire a sound Recordist and a recorder for shooting every time. Therefore the Editor has to dig out effects from the sound library or from any other source. Where there is an action, real sounds are very effective but where there is an expression of human sentiments and sensitivity it is a problem. In such a situation it is always better to use actual sounds whether synchronous or non synchronous. For example in the morning empty roads can be filled with the sounds of morning activities like birds chirping, siren of a factory, morning tunes on the radio etc. can enliven the atmosphere in a dull shot. Similarly in other scenes too creative use of sounds enhance the meaning of visuals. It may be remembered that sounds only complements the visuals, they cannot substitute the visual effects and their meaning. Unlike fictions a documentary films director and editor have to manage the pace and the rhythm of the film with creative editing of disconnected shots and give the film a uniform speed and style. In this job use of experimental sounds and commentary can be very helpful.

Most of the sponsors of Documentary films want that maximum information is given in the shortest possible time thus increasing the dependability on the commentary. Visual become secondary to authenticate the information given in the commentary. Thus these films become a company pamphlet or a booklet. Such films have no artistic or creative merits as the purpose of these films is different but the directors of these films lose an opportunity to make a good film. Directors have ample opportunities to experiment with sounds and other ideas only in documentary films therefore Directors should work more on creative use of sounds than the commentary to let their films not become a piece of a daily news paper which loses its value the very next day.

*****

CUT-7

Glossary

Accelerated Motion: The natural speed of an action in the shot is fastened. It is opposite to 'slow motion'.

Actual Sound: This is the sound which occurs from the actual actions in the scene as actors delivering dialogues, telephone bell, footsteps etc.

Back Projection: When shooting in a studio there is a moving background behind the actors which is projected from a projector kept behind a screen.

Bloop; The triangular shaped Bloop is pasted on the joints to stop unnecessary and irritating 'thud' sound coming from the joints of negative or positive film material.

Bridging Shots: when a continuity jerk is observed between the joints and juxtaposition of two shots, Bridging shots are joined in between the two.

Close Shots: a shot is taken by a camera kept near to the subject or object. Zoom lens is also used to take close shots or medium shots when a subject or object is at a distance.

Camera Angle: an angle to place a camera by which a visual is proposed to be seen.

Cheat Shots: Splitting shots of a dangerous act from a miraculous distance or danger to give a feeling of complete action.

Clap board: A wooden clap board used before a take to give details of the scene, shots and number of takes and clap to synchronize the visual and sound in editing.

Clapper Boy: The person who speaks the details of the scene written on the board and claps before the take.

Close Medium Shot: The shot between close and medium distance generally from knee to head.

Close up: very close to the subject or object to show the details.Generally it is only the face of a person.

Commentary: Explanation or comments running parallel to the visuals.

Commentative sound: The sounds like Back ground music, general atmospheric sounds etc. which are not produced by an action but are felt psychologically along with the scene. Opposite to 'Actual sounds'.

Continuity sheet: A prescribed format which has various columns to be filled with the details of scenes/shots.

Continuity man: The technician who writes about the details of a scene /shot in a prescribed form.

Continuity Title: The caption to link two disconnected scenes for continuity.

Crane shot: Specially designed crane for shooting purposes where a camera is placed to take a shot.

Cross cutting: showing of parallel actions taking place in different locations at the same time to enable the viewers to see both the actions simultaneously one after another without missing the other.

Cutter: The technician who does the physical part of editing.

Cutting Print: The positive print which is used for editing the film. This print is also called the 'Rush print' or 'Rushes'.

Dissolve: Emergence of a shot from the dark with parallel fade out of another one with in the same duration and length gradually. It is decided by parallel markings of fade in and fade out on both the shots on a synchrometer.

Dubbing: It is re recording of dialogues originally recorded on location during shooting. The actors reproduce their dialogues in the basic or any other language in a recording studio.

Dupe Negative: The Duplicate negative which is different from the original negative is made from inter- positive print. This is used to make multiple prints of the film for release purpose.

Duplicate Print: The print made out of the dupe negative.

Establishing shot: It is generally a Long shot used in the beginning to establish the location of the scene.

Effect track: A separate sound track for sound effects in addition to dialogue and music tracks.

Extra shot: The additional shots taken during the shoot.

Fade in: The shot emerge slowly from the dark to full illumination.

Fade out: The fully visible or illuminated shot gradually vanishes in to dark.

Flash back: the scene that takes the viewers to the past. It is used to show a past event or experiences.

Footage: the length of film stripe or a scene measured in feet.

Frame: one of the transparent (Transparency) pictures in the series on the celluloid stripe.

Full shot: Full visual of a subject or object seen in the frame. From head to toe.

Joint: A joint of two celluloid pieces.

Jump: Breaking of the continuity of time and action to proceed to another time and action.

Leader: An ordinary film stripe added before the first frame of the film (Positive or Negative) to thread in the projector/ printing machine. Generally it is a negative film exposed in the sun. There are special leaders for the final film prints and the negatives.

Library shot: the film material not shot for the purpose of a film and preserved separately in the archive or a film library.

Long shot: it is like full shot from head to toe with some additional head space. Long shots also denote wider visual perspective. It is generally used to establish a location or a place.

Married Print: A film print combined with visuals and sound in the same stripe.

Mask: Hiding a portion of a visual seen from the camera. It is done in the camera itself.

Master shot: A shot containing the entire scene in a single shot to guide the editor about the scene. Some directors take master shots for creative purposes.

Medium Shot: Closer than the long shot but away from the range of close shots.

Mixer: An equipment to mix separate sound tracks at the time of rerecording.

Montage: Juxtapositions of disconnected shots to construct a scene with a new meaning.

Multiple exposures: Exposing a frame more than once. It is done to create special visual effects.

Mute Negative: The sound negative which does not contain sound modulations or sound track. It is used to fill the gaps in the sound negative.

Mute print: It is also called 'Silent sound Track (SST) which is used to fill the gaps in the sound positive or 'cutting print' during the editing.

Narrator: A character who explains story or event in a fiction film or a commentator who explains about the scene in non-fiction films.

Optical: Visual effects like dissolve, fades and wipes, super impositions etc. created on a special machine in a film laboratory.

Optical printer: A special machine which creates a scene with the help of a lens and also to make reduction print, special or trick effects.

Over the shoulder: The Camera on the back of the shoulder of a character.

Pan: Moving the camera from left to right or right to left from a fixed position.

Pan Shot: A shot taken by moving camera left and right.

Parallel action: Showing different events occurring at the same time one after another.

Play back: Re play of a pre recorded music track at the time of shooting to synchronize the action with the sound. Play back is generally used for shooting songs and dance sequences.

Post synchronization: Matching of pre recorded sound effects and other sounds with the visuals after the shooting.

Print: Final copy of a film.

Relational Editing: Creating a relationship between the shots during the editing.

Re-recording: Mixing of multiple sound tracks.

Retake: Shooting a shot again.

Rewind, Rewinder: Winding the film rolls on a machine called 'Rewinder'.

Rough cut: First assembly of selected shots to construct a scene.

Slow cutting: Keeping the shots lengthy or for more duration to slow down the pace of the scene. It is reverse of the 'fast cutting.'

Slow motion: Slower than actual speed of an action.

Sound track: on the sides of film stripe the sound modulations or track run parallel to the visuals.

Stock shot: shots preserved in an archive or a film library.

Super impose: Printing of two or more shots on the similar place and length of the film to see them one over another.

Synchronization, Synch: Matching the visuals and sounds parallel to each other so that visuals are seen and sound is heard simultaneously during the projection as if it is coming from the visuals.

Synchronizer: An equipment to synch visuals and sounds in parallel tracks. It can accommodate up to four or six tracks.

Synchronous sounds: The sounds which are synchronized with the visuals or can be synchronized to show the visuals as source of the sounds in the scene.

Take: Recording a shot in the camera.

Tilt: Moving the camera up and down from a fixed position.

Track, Tracking: Moving the camera straight forward or backward on a trolly or any other device. The word 'track' is also used for sound tracks.

Trolley (straight and round): A cart on wheels on which the cameraman sits to take the shot in whatever direction he wants to move.

Truck shot: Shot taken from a truck, trolley, car or any other vehicle.

Wild shooting: Shooting without sound where no sound is recorded with the action.

Wild sound: Recording without visuals. This sound is matched with the scene later.

Wipe: A device to show the transition of the scene like dissolve and fades.

*****

Bibliography

- A Film maker graduated from Film and Television Institute of India, Pune with an experience of over 30 years.
- Written, Produced, Edited & directed more than 200 Short films on variety of subject.
- Author of Books on **'Film Direction', 'Screenplay writing'** and **'Film Editing'** and a coffee table Book on Legendry Play Back Singer of Indian Cinema **Mohammad Rafi: The Melody man**
- Author of anthologies **KASHISH, SISKIYAAN. & DASTAK** of original short stories.
- Authored a Book on Personality Development **GALION SE CHAURAHE TAK.**
- Author of English novels-The Darkness in the Arc, Neither , Behind the moving Images.
- **Editor- Documentary Today** (A magazine on Non-fiction films)
- Rashmin: Marathi Translation of anthology: 'Kashish'
- International Participation in Film festivals-Slovakia, Sweden, Berlin, Rome, Australia, India etc.
- **eBooks on Kindle:**
  -Neither: The Birth of Transgender   (Novel)
  -Behind The Moving Images   (Novel)
  -Elements Of Film Editing   (Cinema)
  - Mohammad Rafi: The Melody Man   (Cinema)

- **International Awards:**
  Non-conventional Energy Resources-Agro Film 84 Slovakia
  Non Conventional Energy Resources- Golden Ear Berlin.1984
  Non Conventional Energy Resources- International consumer film competition-Berlin1985
  Non Conventional Energy Resources- Boris Kidvic Award, International scientific film competition-Belgrade 1985.
  Services of tress-Silver Bunch, International film festival Santarem Portugal 1987
  Watershed Management- F.A.O. Award. slovakia1996
  Poultry Farming- F.A.O. Award, Slovakia 2005.

- **National film Awards:**
  Special Children-Special award 2005
  Hans Akela- Best Biographical film-2008
  Teejan Bai- Best Biographical Film 2002
  Vermiculture-Best Agriculture film 2000
  Tribal Women Artists- Best Art and culture film 2000
  From the land of Buddha to the land of Buddha-Best Historical Reconstruction film 2000
  In search of Excellence - Best Adventure and exploration film. 1998
  Tara Nath Shenoy-Best News Film 1986

- **Other Awards:**
  Police –your friend: Best documentary film, Maharashtra State Award 2002
  Anmol Patthar Bemole Zindagi: Best Documentary film-R.A.P.A. Award 2001

- **Special Honours:**
  - **Scroll of Honours:** for contribution in Indian cinema by Indian organization of mass communication and Institute of Broadcasting Mumbai.
  - **Life Time Achievement Award:** International centre for Cultural Relations, Mumbai.
  - **Hindi Sahitya Samman-** Ministry of Information & Broadcasting, Govt. Of India.
  - **Rajbhasha Shree-** Prasaar Bharti (Govt. Of India) & Ashirwad Award Mumbai.
  - **Saraswat Samman-** Ashirwad Award, Mumbai.

- **Notable Films-**
  - Rafi: We Remember you
  - Toote Pankh
  - Gandhi- an emerging reality
  - Through a lens starkly
  - No Room for fear.
  - Druzhba
  - India-Bhutan Friends forever.

*****

Kuldeep Sinha

www.ingramcontent.com/pod-product-compliance
Lightning Source LLC
Chambersburg PA
CBHW072301200526
45168CB00014B/122